P9-CKR-226

Other Ways to
win

In memory of Jennifer Carter Gray

Second Edition

Other Ways to
Win

*Creating
Alternatives
for High School
Graduates*

Kenneth C. Gray
Edwin L. Herr

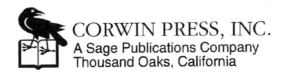

CORWIN PRESS, INC.
A Sage Publications Company
Thousand Oaks, California

For information:

Corwin Press, Inc.
A Sage Publications Company
2455 Teller Road
Thousand Oaks, California 91320
E-mail: order@corwinpress.com

Sage Publications Ltd.
6 Bonhill Street
London EC2A 4PU
United Kingdom

Sage Publications India Pvt. Ltd.
M-32 Market
Greater Kailash I
New Delhi 110 048 India

Printed in the United States of America

Library of Congress Cataloging-in-Publication Data

Gray, Kenneth C.
  Other ways to win : Creating alternatives for high school graduates /
by Kenneth C. Gray, Edwin L. Herr.— 2nd ed.
        p. cm.
Includes bibliograph ical references and index.
  ISBN 0-7619-7568-3 (cloth : alk. paper)
  ISBN 0-7619-7569-1 (pbk. : alk. paper)
  1. Career education—United States. 2. High school
students—Vocational guidance—United States. 3. High school
graduates—Employment—United States. 4. Postsecondary
education—United States. 5. High school graduates—United
States—Social conditions. I. Herr, Edwin L. II. Title.
  LC1037.5 .G73 2000
  370.11'3'0973—dc21   00-008377

This book is printed on acid-free paper.

00   01   02   03   04   05   10   9   8   7   6   5   4   3   2   1

Corwin Editorial Assistant: Catherine Kantor
Production Editor: Denise Santoyo
Editorial Assistant: Victoria Cheng
Typesetter/Designer: Danielle Dillahunt
Cover Designer: Oscar Desierto

Contents

Preface to the Second Edition   xi
Preface to the First Edition   xiii
    Acknowledgments   xiv
About the Authors   xv

PART I: THE *ONE WAY TO WIN* MENTALITY

1. Rescuing a Generation Adrift   3

SECTION I: The *One Way to Win* Paradigm Explained   4
    The Result: College Mania   7

SECTION II: The Costs of *One Way to Win*   7
    The Human Cost of *One Way to Win*   10
    The Costs of Skill Shortages:
       The Quiet National Dilemma   12
    Technical Skill Shortages   13
    The Importance of Technically Skilled Workers   13
    A Case Study: Keith and the College Game   15
    Other Ways to Win   16

2. Recognizing the Forces Behind *One Way to Win*   17
    Understanding the *One Way to Win* Mentality   18

SECTION I: The Pressure to Go to College
From Parents and Others   20
    Pressure From Parents   20

Pressure From High Schools 22

Pressure From Peers and the Media 24

SECTION II: The Economic and Social Forces
Behind *One Way to Win* 25

Diminishing Economic Opportunities 25

Labor Market Misconceptions 26

The True Concern of Teens and Parents 27

Social Class and Status 28

The Prejudice Against Nonprofessional Work 29

The Ideology of Equal Opportunity 30

SECTION III: The Enablers Behind *One Way to Win:*
Open Admissions and Financial Aid 32

Open College Admissions 33

Nonmerit Financial Aid 34

Other Ways to Win 34

3. **Limited Options for Special Populations** 36

SECTION I: Economically Disadvantaged Youth 37

SECTION II: Women and the Gender Wage Gap 40

Other Ways to Win 43

**PART II: COUNTING THE LOSERS
IN THE *ONE WAY TO WIN* GAME**

4. **Questionable Academic Preparation** 47

SECTION I: How Effective Is the College Prep
Program of Study? 48

The College Prep Program and the
Academically Average 49

The Class of 1998 Follow-Up Study 52

Going to College: Do Academic
Credentials Matter? 54

SECTION II: The High School Experience of
Those in the Academic Middle 56

College Prep Course-Taking Patterns 56

Other Ways to Win 61

5. **Winners and Losers in the *One Way to Win* Game** 63

SECTION I: Remedial Education and College Dropouts:
The First Losers 64

Academic Ability to Benefit   64
Remedial Education in Higher Education   65
College Dropouts   67

SECTION II: Underemployed College Graduates:
The Second Losers   70
     The Labor Market Outlook for College Graduates   71

SECTION III: More Losers? Those Who Prepare for
College but Go to Work Instead   75
     Dead-End Jobs for Those Without Vocational
     Education   75
     Other Ways to Win   77

6. **Who Cares? The Politics of Average Students**   **79**

SECTION I: High School Politics and the
Academically Average   80
     Why High School Educators Look the Other Way   82
     Are Guidance Counselors the Villains?   83
     Grade Inflation   84
     The Stalemate in High School Classrooms   84

SECTION II: Taking the High Ground:
The Role of Elected Officials   86

SECTION III: Behind the Scenes:
Those With Vested Interests   87
     Other Ways to Win   88

PART III: CREATING *OTHER WAYS TO WIN*

7. **The High Skill/High Wage Rationale**   **93**

SECTION I: Five Misconceptions About
the Future Labor Market   94

SECTION II: The High Skill/High Wage Rationale
for Creating *Other Ways to Win*   99
     Examples of Prebaccalaureate High Skill/
         High Wage Occupations   100
     Occupational Outlook for High Skill/High Wage
         Occupations Not Requiring a Baccalaureate
         Degree   103
     Opportunities for Special Populations   106

Importance of Occupational Skill and
    Postsecondary Technical Education   107
Five Points to Make With Parents   108
Other Ways to Win   109

8. **Step 1: Providing Systematic Career Guidance
for Students and Structured Feedback for Parents**   **110**

SECTION I: Systematic Career Guidance
   for All Students   111
   Career Choices and Postsecondary Success   112
   Systematic Career Guidance Defined   113
   The Problem of Adolescent Career Immaturity   115
   The Individual Career Plan   119
   Career Pathways/Career Majors/
     Career Academies   121

SECTION II: Providing Feedback to Parents   123
   Delivering the Wake-Up Call to Parents   124
   A Four-Step Parental Involvement Program   125
   Five Points to Make With Parents   129
   Other Ways to Win   131

9. **Step 2: Redesigning the High School
Academic Curriculum**   **133**

SECTION I: The Current Status of the
   College Prep Program   134
   A Proposal for the Redesign of the
     Academic Curriculum   135
   Two New Transitional Emphases   140
   Postsecondary Placement Services for All   148

SECTION II: The New Role of High School Career
   and Technical Education   149
   Other Ways to Win   152

10. **Step 3: Ensuring Equal Status and Focused Academics**   **153**

SECTION I: Putting an End to Taylorism   154
   Defining Taylorism   155
   Taylorist Influences on High Schools   156
   Challenging the Taylorist Rationale   157
   Strategies for Ending Taylorism   159

SECTION II: Modifying Instructional Modalities
  and Practices   162
    Matching Instruction and Learning Styles   163
SECTION III: Motivating the Academic Middle   168
    Strategies for Motivating the Majority   169
    Other Ways to Win   171

11. Bringing "Average" Students to Excellence   **172**
    Challenging the *One Way to Win* Paradigm   174
    There Are *Other Ways to Win*   176
    Reaching Out to Parents   178
    Career Development/Guidance for All Students   179
    Redesigning the Academic Prep Program   180
    Challenging the High School Culture   182
    Doing What's Right   184

References   **186**

Index   **191**

Preface to the Second Edition

This second edition of *Other Ways to Win* was prompted by the many requests from readers of the original. They wondered in particular if there were more recent statistics regarding other ways for teens—in the academic middle—to win. Thus, new data have replaced old where necessary and possible. We have also modified some of our observations and recommendations as a result of both changing times and discussions with educators across the nation.

Alas, we had wished that the plight of the academic middle would be greatly improved and a second edition of *Other Ways to Win* would not be necessary. But, although progress has been made, the need to spread the *other ways to win* message still exists. Teens from the academic middle still need a lot of help; all too many are still heading off to college, thinking it is the only way to win, and the success rate among those who do is still one in four. But there are other, better, alternatives. . . . If you don't believe it, read on!

—Ken Gray
—Edwin Herr

Preface to the First Edition

Having worked earlier in our careers as both high school teachers and counselors, we enjoy being in high schools, particularly at the beginning or end of any high school day, as students file in and out of the building. It is always fascinating to see the diversity, fashions, and interpersonal dramas that are played out. It always leaves us with a feeling of wellness, that the future is in good hands. Well, at least it used to.

During the past 10 years, we have found ourselves worrying more and more about high school-aged adolescents as they approach graduation. Not all of them, of course; in particular, not the top 25% or 30%, the academically blessed, who seem to have everything going for them. We are concerned about the fate of the rest, particularly those from the academic middle. We worry because these adolescents face a difficult and uncertain labor market. We worry because they have been told there is only *one way to win*, namely, to prepare for the professional ranks by going to a 4-year college. Unfortunately, although this career advice is realistic for some high school students, it is clearly unrealistic for many of them. Particularly for many of those from the academic middle, this advice is totally out of sync both with their high school academic records and with the labor market they will face if they actually graduate with a 4-year college degree.

Tragically, for these students, the only certainty is that the majority will accumulate significant student loan debt in the process.

Thus, we wrote this book for those in the academic middle of our high school classes, their parents, and their teachers—to alert them to an important fact: There are *other ways to win* in today's labor market. Our intent is not necessarily to dissuade students from attempting a 4-year college program; rather, it is to point out alternatives that carry, for many, a higher probability of success, as well as lower tuition costs. We argue that the key to future economic security is not education per se, but rather obtaining the occupational skills that lead to high skill/high wage work. Whereas some of these skills are typically learned in 4-year colleges or graduate schools, others can be learned at 1- or 2-year postsecondary technical institutions, and still others can be learned in work-based programs sponsored by employers and employee groups.

This book is divided into three parts. In Part I, the *one way to win* belief is explored in detail. In Part II, the secondary and post-secondary experiences of those in the academic middle are analyzed in order to document the frequent failure of those who attempt a 4-year college degree program to either complete a degree or attain a professional job. In Part III, we outline three major steps and various strategies that high school educators can take to modify the high school program in order to create *other ways to win* for those in the academic middle. We hope, ultimately, to create advocates for the academically average and to bring them into the mainstream of educational reform debates.

Acknowledgments

Many individuals have made this book possible, beginning with Alice Foster of Corwin Press, who urged the consideration of the project in the first place. We wish to acknowledge in particular the contributions of Tammy Fetterolf and Lee Carpenter for providing the word processing and editing, and to all those, too numerous to name, whose encouragement regarding the importance of the topic kept the project moving along. Our thanks to you all.

About the Authors

Kenneth C. Gray is Professor in the Workforce Education and Development Program at Pennsylvania State University, Main Campus. He holds a BA in Economics from Colby College, an MA in Counseling Psychology from Syracuse University, and a doctorate in Technical Education from Virginia Tech. Prior to joining the faculty at Penn State, he was Superintendent of the Vocational Technical High School System in Connecticut and has been a high school English teacher, guidance counselor, and administrator. He has published widely and is frequently quoted in the national press. He is co-author with Edwin Herr of the text, *Workforce Education: The Basic*. His latest book, *Getting Real: Helping Teens Find Their Future*, addresses the importance of helping teenagers develop career direction as a prerequisite to postsecondary success.

Edwin L. Herr is Distinguished Professor of Education (Counselor Education and Counseling Psychology) and Associate Dean for Graduate Programs, Research and Technology, College of Education, Pennsylvania State University. He received his BS degree in Business Education from Shippensburg State College, and an MA and EdD in Counseling and Student Personnel Administration from Teachers College, Columbia University, where he was an Alumni Fellow. A former business teacher, school counselor, and director of guidance, he previously served as Assistant and Associate Professor of Counselor Education at the State University of New York at Buffalo (1963-1966) and as the First Director of the Bureau of Guidance

Services and the Bureau of Pupil Personnel Services, Pennsylvania
Department of Education (1966-1968). The author or coauthor of
more than 250 articles and 28 books and monographs, he is Past President of the American Association for Counseling and Development,
Past President of the National Vocational Guidance Association, and
Past President of the Association for Counselor Education and Supervision. He has been elected a Fellow of the American Psychological Association, the American Psychological Society, and the American Association for Applied and Preventive Psychology for his
"unique and sustained contributions to psychology." Among his
many awards, he has received the Eminent Career Award of the National Career Development Association.

1
The *One Way to Win* Mentality

1

Rescuing a Generation Adrift

How beautiful is youth, how bright it gleams
With its illusions, aspirations, and dreams.
Longfellow, "Morituri Salutamus"
(1807-1887)

ach year, U.S. high schools graduate roughly 2.8 million
students, almost 75% of all youth aged 17. Think back to
the last high school graduation you remember—the
long line of graduates in caps and gowns, some jubilant, some cry-
ing, most just silent and pensive. Among them were the students
who were academically special, the ones everyone knew, the so-
called future leaders: the class valedictorian, the national honor society members, the honor roll students. This book is not about most of
them. It is about many of the rest—the "forgotten" or "academic"
middle. These academically average students are the adolescents
who, seeing no other alternatives, typically head off to a 4-year college or a 2-year transfer college despite being academically and/or
emotionally ill prepared for the experience. The tragedy is that many
are not successful and as a result drop out. Even among those who
graduate, as many as one half may never find college-level work.

Both the academically blessed and the academic middle, however, have one thing in common: They will spend a lot of money, and
most will end up with significant student loan debt however long

they attend college. This situation makes little sense, and the costs of this folly are getting out of hand. These youth are adrift in an uncertain world. They see only *one way to win* the race for the American dream. The likelihood that they will win is slim, yet they see little choice because we have failed to prepare them for legitimate alternatives. This situation requires correction. This book's focus is on the creation of these alternatives by reengineering the high school program of study.

The word *adrift* connotes visions of floundering, uncertainty, lack of control, and ultimate peril. It accurately describes a large percentage of today's high school students—students whose aspirations and postsecondary plans are inconsistent with both their high school academic record and labor market projections. These youth exhibit all the classic signs of career immaturity: Their plans are inconsistent with reality; they are floundering; and ultimately many are disappointed or even scarred by their experiences. Who are these students? Typically, they are thought to be mostly the noncollege-bound. Not so. The majority of even academically average high school students now go to college. In fact, the most visible sign of mass confusion among the nation's youth is the growing percentage of high school graduates who enroll in 4-year colleges or 2-year programs that transfer to a 4-year degree program. Why do they go? Because they have been taught that there is now only *one way to win*.

SECTION I

The *One Way to Win* Paradigm Explained

The "one way to win" mentality is best explained by expressed views of teens themselves. Such insights can be gained from the annual national survey of college freshman (American Council on Education, 1999), as well as survey and other data from the National Center for Education Statistics (NCES). The "one way to win" paradigm has three conventional wisdoms:

❑ Wisdom 1: Go to college to get a 4-year degree.

Within 2 years of graduating from high school, 72% of graduates have enrolled in higher education. Ninety-five percent of college

TABLE 1.1 College Freshmen: Reasons Noted as Very Important in Deciding to Go to College

	Total (%)	Men(%)	Women (%)
To get a better job	77	77	77
To make more money	75	79	72
To learn about things that interest me	62	56	67
To prepare for graduate school	49	43	55
Parents wanted me to go	40	37	41

SOURCE: Compiled from *American Freshman National Norms for Fall 1998* by the American Council on Education, 1994a, Washington, DC: Author.

freshman in the 1998 American Freshman Survey, for example, had just graduated from high school that same year. One might expect that at least half would be pursuing 1- or 2-year associate degrees. Not so! Two thirds indicate that they plan to earn bachelor's degrees immediately and 95% eventually. Only 4% indicated that they plan to study in technical areas at the prebaccalaureate 1- and 2-year level; only 1% of women so indicated.

❑ Wisdom 2: Why? To get a high-paying job.

Most young adults are in college in hopes that it will lead to future economic gain—economists call it "labor market advantage." Table 1.1 indicates the results of asking college freshman what were important reasons for matriculating. Arguably, three of the top four are economic reasons. Number 1 is get a better job, and it is equally important to young women and men. Number 2 is to earn more money. A distant third is to gain a general education. A somewhat startling 49% of freshman already foresee the need to go to graduate school.

❑ Wisdom 3: Where? In the professional ranks.

TABLE 1.2 Percentage of High School Seniors in 1972 and 1992
Who Expected to Be Employed in Various
Occupations, by Gender

Occupation	All Seniors		Males		Females	
	1972	1992	1972	1992	1972	1992
Clerical	14.2	3.5	1.9	1.2	25.5	5.7
Craftperson/Trade	7.5	2.8	15.1	5.3	0.5	0.3
Farming	1.6	1.0	2.7	1.6	0.6	0.4
Homemaker	3.1	1.2	0.0	0.1	5.9	2.2
Laborer	2.5	0.8	4.9	1.4	0.3	0.1
Manager	3.1	6.0	5.1	6.6	1.3	5.4
Military	2.4	3.2	4.1	5.6	0.8	0.8
Operative	2.3	1.2	3.9	2.1	0.8	0.2
Professional	45.4	59.0	41.8	49.3	48.8	68.8
Proprietor	1.8	6.7	3.2	8.7	0.5	4.8
Protective services	2.2	4.1	4.2	6.9	0.4	1.4
Sales	3.0	1.9	2.7	2.3	3.3	1.5
Service	4.2	2.6	1.6	0.6	6.7	4.6
Technical	6.6	6.0	8.8	8.4	4.6	3.7
Total	100.0	100.0	100.0	100.0	100.0	100.0

SOURCES: Compiled from *National Longitudinal Study, 1972 (base year),* by
the National Center for Education Statistics, 1972, Washington, DC: U.S.
Department of Education; and *National Educational Longitudinal Study of
1988, 1992 Second Follow-Up,* by the National Center for Education
Statistics, 1992, Washington, DC: U.S. Department of Education.

NOTE: Percentages may not add to 100 due to rounding.

When asked what job they would like to have by the time they
are 30, overwhelmingly high school students pick professional occupations (see Table 1.2). About half of all young men and more than
two thirds of all young women surveyed as high school seniors pick
professional occupations. Only 8% of males and 4% of females indicated aspirations in technical occupations. In a period of significant
and growing skill shortages in skilled blue/gold-collar occupations,

it is noteworthy that only 5% of males and virtually no females (0.3%) expected to be employed in craftspersons/trade careers.

The Result: College Mania

With this final piece of information about high school graduates' career plans, the "operational definition" of the *one way to win* paradigm is complete. *The one way to win paradigm is the belief that the only hope for future economic security for today's youth is at least a 4-year college degree obtained with the expectation that it will lead to a good-paying job in the professions.* The extent to which all high school graduates appear to be internalizing the *one way to win* paradigm and basing their future plans on it, regardless of their abilities, academic preparation, or labor market realities, is truly astonishing; it has reached manic proportions.

The dictionary defines *mania* as "excessive or unreasonable enthusiasm" (*Merriam-Webster's*, 1993, p. 707). The current enthusiasm for a 4-year college degree is excessive and therefore "manic" in nature.

It is excessive because it is expressed without regard to academic ability, maturity, or a well-thought-out reason for matriculating. Although most teens indicate that they want to go to college to get a good-paying job, very few have taken the time to think about the details. Most aspire to the professional ranks, yet professional work is only 20% of all employment in the United States; meanwhile, less than 5% aspire to technical careers, which is the fastest-growing segment of high-skills employment in the economy. In fact, many teens go to college because they have no idea what they want to do or what options are available other than attending a 4-year baccalaureate degree program. Higher education, particularly at the university level, has become the default decision for today's youth and their parents as well.

SECTION II

The Costs of *One Way to Win*

For the academically blessed (the top 30%—those who attend the so-called medallion or prestigious colleges), the *one way to win* paradigm makes sense; the rest would be wise to at least consider other alternatives, and the nation would be wise to provide and value these alternatives. Wise because there are financial and psychological costs associated with trying the *one way to win* strategy. Because of these costs, pursuing the *one way to win* paradigm is not benign for students. It is not like trying out for the senior play or some athletic team in high school. On the contrary, pursuing the *one way to win* plan is very costly. First of all, it is expensive to students, parents, and taxpayers. Second, three out of four who try the plan FAIL; either they fail to graduate or they fail to find employment commensurate with their degree. Finally, there are the economic development costs that result from a mismatch between good opportunities in the workforce and the skills/credentials, or lack thereof, of today's young adults. In this section these costs are discussed further.

The most obvious and perhaps the only publicized costs of the *one way to win* mentality and the related phenomenon of "college mania" are those that can be measured in dollars and cents. These costs arise from charges for tuition, room, board, books, transportation, junior year abroad, and so forth. They accrue to both students and parents, but also to government—by way of the taxpayer.

This latter point is important. Were those pursuing the *one way to win* paradigm spending their own money, perhaps the negative results would not be a matter of public concern. However, except for the very few students who pay the full cost at the very few private colleges with huge endowments, every student in higher education is subsidized to varying degrees by the taxpaying public. Thus, the true cost of college mania is of concern to everyone, including those who do not have children in college. But first, let us examine the costs to students and parents alone.

The Costs to Students and Parents

The *one way to win* mentality that has gripped the nation might not be a concern—or at least as much of a concern—if it were easily affordable to students and parents. In reality, however, and despite efforts by higher education to debunk the truth, college is costly; college costs continue to increase at rates higher than inflation. Between 1986 and 1996, tuition, room, and board increased 20% at public institutions and 31% at private. More important is the ability of families to pay. To paraphrase NCES research (1998), after a period of decline in the 1960s and 1970s, tuition, room, and board rose to 15% of family income in 1993 at public institutions and 42% at private. And, although this rate has remained relatively stable, for a family at the 10th percentile of family income, it amounts to 32% and 88%, respectively.

A second reality of higher education cost is that now one half of all students need financial aid. In many public and private universities, it is more like two thirds. More important, financial aid is today just a code word for debt. Whereas in the 1970s and even the early 1980s only a small part of a student loan package was loans, now it is closer to two thirds. As an indicator, 52% of college seniors in the mid-1990s borrowed money for college; the average student loan debt at graduation was $11,000 at public and $13,200 at private institutions (NCES, 1998, Indicator 14).

The Costs to the Public

Although the rising cost of higher education for students and parents is well publicized, the cost to the taxpaying public through government aid to institutions and students is not. At public institutions, state and federal governments pay the largest part of the costs. Federal and state appropriations/grants and contracts account for 62% of revenues at public universities and 65% at public 4-year colleges. This does not include financial aid to students; the federal government alone allocates about $20 billion for financial assistance and guaranteed student loans. These expenditures have, for a long time, gone unquestioned. No longer!

Particularly at the state level, elected officials are beginning to ask what they are getting for multibillion-dollar investment in higher education and student financial aid. If the goal is to provide opportunities for graduates, how much opportunity is being created as indicated by job placement? If the goal is to stimulate economic growth, are the degrees awarded consistent with the labor market needs of the state?

When state officials look, they typically find all the predicted results of the *one way to win* mania. Specifically, they find that (a) the vast majority of enrollment is in 4-year degree programs or 2-year general studies transfer programs, (b) graduation rates are 50% or lower, (c) growing percentages of graduates are underemployed, and (d) the degrees awarded are out of sync with the economic development needs of the state. As a result, a few states are implementing performance funding (Schmidt, 1999), which is based on graduation rates, employment rates, and successful certificate exams passed.

In summary, the financial costs of the *one way to win* mania are significant whether one is a student, a parent, or a taxpayer. But the issue of dollars and cents masks what may be the most dangerous cost of the *one way to win* mentality. A more menacing threat may well be the long-term human costs that accrue to those who try but lose.

The Human Cost of *One Way to Win*

A less-publicized but more insidious and cruel human cost results from the *one way to win* mentality and college mania. To illustrate the human cost of providing only *one way to win*, we have created a little parable about a faraway place where there was also only *one way to win*: by jumping 6-foot fences!

The High-Jump Parable

A long time ago, in a place far away, there was a group of people who valued above all, fairness, equity, and social justice. Unfortunately, like everywhere else, there was not quite enough wealth to go around; thus, distribution of wealth was always a problem. It seemed that no matter what was tried, the children of the wealthy ended up wealthy and the children of the poor ended up poor. Finally, the leaders decided on a new system. There would be a single standard, one that was independent of family wealth and other variables related to wealth. The single standard was jumping over a 6-foot fence.

Now the leaders thought they were on to something with this new standard. It was objective. Everyone could try. High jumping had nothing to do with one's background. Those who made it over the 6-foot fence were given the better jobs, therefore wealth; those who did not were given the poorer jobs or no jobs at all and were poor. They expected that everyone would be happy. Thus, the leaders were confused when, after a very short time, most were not happy at all.

The trouble stemmed from the fact that the single standard was not fair to all. First, jumping over a 6-foot hurdle was easy for some people because they were born with long or extra springy legs that made high jumping easy, not because these people worked harder than others. Thus, this group gained status and wealth, not because of merit, but because of the fortunes of birth after all. This had not been the leaders' intention.

Even among those who could leap 6 feet, many were unhappy. Why? Because the economy of the high-jump culture had not been very good: There were not enough high-paying jobs for all who could jump 6 feet; in short, the promise of economic security could not be kept.

According to the leadership advisers, however, a bigger problem than those who could jump 6 feet but did not get the promised jobs and wealth, were those from the middle ranks of high jumpers. These borderline jumpers believed or were led to believe that they could jump 6 feet if they took the right training program in high school, the so-called high-jump prep curriculum. Most borderline jumpers enrolled in this curriculum and even took the special high-jumping aptitude test designed to predict their ability to ever clear 6 feet. This tactic did not matter much, however, because regardless of their performance on this high-jumping test or in the high-jump prep curriculum, just about everyone was allowed to enroll in the post-high school high-jump contest anyway.

Unfortunately, attending these contests was very expensive. Wanting everything to be fair, the leaders arranged for loans for those unable to afford the program. Of the students in this group, some eventually jumped 6 feet, but fewer than half did so. Most of the borderline high jumpers gave up and drifted home, defeated and burdened with debt.

The advisers to the leader of the high-jump culture were wise men and women. Thus, they warned that the real tragedy affected those youth who determined early in life that they were never going to jump 6 feet because they had short legs and lead feet. This group was the unhappiest of all. Many either dropped out of high school or came to school but did not pay much attention; after all, why should they—in a culture whose only valued accomplishment was jumping 6 feet? Clearly, they would not achieve this.

Having heard this report, the leaders were deeply troubled; it was obvious that what they had viewed as fair—this single standard—was not fair at all. Most who tried to jump 6 feet failed and, in the process, lost both confidence and their money. The most harmful aspect was that some had no hope of ever jumping 6 feet and thus gave up early in life.

This attitude caused the leaders to ask the obvious question: "What should we do?" "Easy," said the advisers. "Create *other ways to win.*" Alternatives could include learning to build and maintain technology and mastering academic skills. These alternatives could lead to high status and, if the economy improved, to higher earnings. Thus, new options were added. The high-jump culture evolved into the "many ways to win" culture. Many more people tried, and more actually won. The culture changed from one in which most lost and became embittered to one in which hope prevailed and sufficient options were available. Almost everyone had a legitimate hope of succeeding in at least one option and enjoying the rewards.

This parable of the high-jump culture illustrates the theme of this book: the need for and benefits of creating *other ways to win.* The parallels between the current U.S. culture and this hypothetical nation of high jumpers are obvious. At present in the United States, youth only have *one way to win.* In the parable, this was the ability to jump 6 feet; in our culture, it is getting a baccalaureate degree. Unfortunately, evidence presented in the next chapters shows that the baccalaureate degree route is not for everyone. We need to be as wise as the leaders' advisers and realize that the *one way to win* mentality hurts many who have no hope of ever entering the game; these individuals deserve other options. But before moving on to further develop this topic, we should note one other cost or threat imposed by the *one way to win* mentality: (a) the serious mismatch it causes between the types of skills that will be needed by the United States to be economically competitive and (b) the aspirations of U.S. youth.

The Costs of Skill Shortages: The Quiet National Dilemma

By the mid-1990s, a quiet national dilemma had developed in the United States that is predicted to persist: There was an unprecedented shortage of skilled technicians while, at the same time, there were growing percentages of underemployed 4-year college graduates. Underemployment is discussed in detail in Chapter 5, Section

II. Here we discuss the impact of skill shortages on the ability of the nation to maximize its economic advantage.

Technical Skill Shortages

The 1990s proved to be a time of dramatic economic growth in the United States. Between 1991 and 1996, the gross domestic product increased from $4.9 trillion to $7.6 trillion, with an inflation rate of only 2.9%. As the end of the decade approached, however, serious labor shortages developed.

The term *labor shortage* does not accurately reflect the situation. The shortage was not of high school graduates or those with bachelor's or graduate degrees, nor of engineers or scientists, but of technicians trained at the postsecondary prebaccalaureate level. Be it information technology industries, precision manufacturing, electronics production, or building construction, virtually all industries that employed technical workers—workers who used mathematics and science principles to make decisions on the job—were facing shortages. In some instances, employers were using headhunters and offering bonuses to identify and recruit technicians—techniques previously reserved for selected 4-year college graduates.

The Importance of
Technically Skilled Workers

By the late 1990s, the ability of the United States to fully maximize the economic advantage it then had over less well-performing European and Pacific Rim economies was seriously hindered by the lack of technicians. The Hudson Institute (Judy & Dí Amico, 1997) predicted that, unless the skills gap was closed, the gross domestic product (GDP) could be negatively affected by as much as 5%.

At the state and local level, it became apparent that economic development and plant expansion and relocation now hinged primarily on the availability of technicians trained at the postsecondary 1- and 2-year levels, or those holding specialized occupational certificates such as Novel, Cisco Systems, or Microsoft. A company could usually find unskilled or semiskilled individuals who could be trained on the job in a matter or days and, if it needed engineers, there was a worldwide glut in all but a few specialties. The problem was finding technicians. To quote a study done by the Pennsylvania Economy League (1996), "A region that does not have a growing percentage of its 'non-professional' workforce trained at the post-secondary pre-baccalaureate level will face increasing difficulty attracting and keeping high valued added employment" (p. i).

The reality of such predictions is illustrated by a study of the impact of labor shortages on one Pennsylvania county (Passmore, Wall, & Harvey, 1996). The inability of one firm in this county to hire 30 precision machinists required it to curtail expansion plans. This curtailment, in turn, led to a direct and indirect countywide loss of $20 million in economic output and $3 million in tax revenue. Unable to fill technician and other skilled jobs, employers across the nation turned to the Congress, asking that the number of H-1B immigration visas be increased in order to recruit internationally for skilled workers. Congress had to agree.

How did such a skills mismatch develop? Predictably, the schools, both high schools and colleges, were the first to be blamed.

The consensus was that they simply were not turning out sufficient numbers of people with the necessary skills. Such charges missed the point. The problem is not that students do not have the technical skills, it's that they all want to be professionals. The shortage of technicians may be ascribed to the simple reality that, among those with the necessary talent, few are interested because (a) they have been told that there is only *one way to win* and (b) few know anything about other opportunities. Statistics regarding college enrollment confirm this view.

Between 1985 and 1997, the number of BS degrees in engineering in the United States fell 16%; computer science and math degrees fell 29%. Only 12% of all degrees awarded in the country are in technical areas. But is this the fault of the nation's schools and colleges? Hardly! In the Pennsylvania county mentioned above, a precision manufacturing training program existed but was on the verge of closing because of a lack of student interest. Forty-eight percent of all PhD graduates in technical fields in the United States are foreigners; universities admit these students because American youth are either not interested or not willing to make the sacrifice of time and hard work required to complete these degrees.

The skill gap that developed in the 1990s is the result of many factors. The fundamental problem is the *one way to win* mentality that causes many poor decisions by young adults. As argued previously, today's youth are not just making bad decisions; most are going to college by default—as if it were just the 5th year of high school.

The shortage of technicians trained at the prebaccalaureate level will not disappear until the nation's youth choose to pursue careers in areas of high technical demand. In the United States, government has neither the power nor the will to mandate these decisions. It is up to the individual. The only hope is that teens will make better choices when better informed, when the myth of the *one way to win* mentality is exposed, and when technical education becomes valued. The purpose of this book is to assist those who would take on such a task. However, should there still be any doubt about the need, this chapter ends by relating a student interview conducted as part of the research for this book.

A Case Study

Keith and the College Game

Keith was 17. His high school academic record was mediocre at best; at the time of the interview, he was not certain he had enough credits to be offically called a senior. His principal ambition was to obtain his driver's license, which he did not have because he lacked the academic skills and ability to pass the "rules of the road" part of the driver's test. During the interview, he was asked about his postgraduation plans. The interviewer expected a reply about the need to find full-time employment; instead, Keith said, "I haven't decided yet what college to go to. I'll decide next year." The interviewer was speechless. Keith responded with a glare that said, "Did you believe me?"—a look familiar to those who work in high schools.

The gulf between Keith's abilities and his stated postgraduation plans leads one to conclude that this young man was seriously adrift; fantasy is an inadequate description of his plans. Then again, perhaps he wasn't fantasizing; perhaps he was just playing the game, saying what he thought the interviewer, like his peers and possibly his parents, wanted to hear. Perhaps he really knew that college was not a viable option for him. At any rate, not long thereafter, Keith left school and left home. He may have realized the folly of the idea of going to college and decided to spare himself the embarrassment—a

hint of the human cost of providing only *one way to win*. He and literally millions like him—most of whom are blessed with considerably
more academic ability—see only *one way to win*. These teens call this
situation "the college game." "College mania" seems more appropriate. There needs to be more than one game, as well as *other ways to
win*.

Other Ways to Win

We have argued in this chapter that many of today's graduating
high school seniors, particularly those from the academic middle,
are seriously adrift. They have been led to believe that a baccalaureate degree will lead to a career in the professions and is the only way
to ensure future economic security and status. This mentality, in
turn, has fueled college mania—the unfounded enthusiasm for a 4-
year degree. Unfortunately, the *one way to win* paradigm is a myth,
and college mania is not benign—it has significant costs to the
United States and to its youth. Most devastating, it has caused many
youth to give up hope. This mania is a cancer on the nation. Like any
disease, its pathology must be understood before a cure can be developed. This analysis is the purpose of Chapter 2.

2

Recognizing the Forces
Behind *One Way to Win*

*It's gotten to the point where each person should be issued a college
diploma [at birth] instead of a birth certificate.*
A. Shanker (1994, p. 4)[1]

The vast majority of today's high school students who populate the academic middle are acting out career plans that are clearly unrealistic and that stem from the *one way to win* mentality. Having been taught that there is only one road to the American dream, the majority (94.7%) express the intent to continue their education; most (83.9%) want a degree from a 4-year college, and most (57% of men and 74% of women) say they will seek jobs in the professional ranks (NCES,1992). For many, particularly those in the academic middle, these plans are clearly fantasy: Unless U.S. high schools suddenly become so instructionally effective that 84% graduate with the requisite skills to complete a baccalaureate degree and unless the structure of the future labor market changes dramatically to provide twice as much professional work, they have no realistic reason to expect to achieve these goals.

Meanwhile, the costs of this fantasy for the United States, its youth, and their parents are increasing. These costs are high both in terms of their negative impact on the nation's future competitiveness and on personal, federal, and state budgets, and in terms of the human cost of limited opportunities, unmet expectations, and resulting pessimism, cynicism, and low self-esteem. If the damage done by the *one way to win* mentality is to be undone and if its costs are to be brought under control, the factors that make this ideology so pervasive must be understood. That is the purpose of this chapter.

Understanding the
One Way to Win Mentality

Although the magnitude and effectiveness of the current pressure or "press" to go to college (see Figure 2.1) may be historic, the factors that influence youths' decisions to attend higher education have been of interest to researchers for some time. For example, Hossler and Stage (1992) developed a statistically valid model for the "predisposition" to go to college. This model explains the decision as a reaction to parental/peer pressure coupled with an individual's academic ability or high school record. Pressure from parents and peers, in turn, results from pressures applied from social messages and morals, as well as conventional economic wisdom. Using the Hossler and Stage model as a starting point, we offer an expanded model to explain the factors that make the *one way to win* philosophy so prevalent in the 1990s.

In our college choice model, the decision stems from ubiquitous pressure to go to college; this pressure comes from parents, friends, teachers, and the media. The consistent message from all of these groups is that there is only *one way to win*: Go to a 4-year college and pursue a career in the professions. If one believes, as we do, that persons promoting the *one way to win* mentality are well intentioned and sincerely believe in this advice, then one must assume that their beliefs are based on a rationale that comes from some rather convincing economic arguments, from deep-seated ideologies and values, or from both. In our model, we suggest three such variables: economic uncertainty, social status, and the ideology of equity and the right to fail.

Academic skills are conspicuously missing from the factors that we argue fuel college mania. This was not an oversight. In these times of excess capacity in higher education and resultant open admissions at all but a small fraction of 4-year colleges, academic abil-

Figure 2.1 The "Push" to Go to College

NOTE: Illustration by Denise Dorricott.

ity no longer seems to be a consideration in the decision to pursue a 4-year college degree. Although academic ability may well determine which 4-year college a student will attend, lack of academic ability no longer means not going.

Thus we view open admissions and financial aid based on need and not academic skills as the two most important factors that facilitate college mania. They do not cause it, but they make it possible. One reason for the popularity of the *one way to win* mantra is that there are no obstacles to trying it. Open admissions have given virtually all a seat in higher education regardless of academic skills. National polls indicate that the American public believes everyone who is "qualified" should be able to go to college. It is doubtful, however, that many understand that their tax dollars are being used to ensure that all who are not qualified can go as well.

In the rest of this chapter, the causes and enablers of the *one way to win* mentality are discussed. We begin with a discussion of the pressures applied on teens by parents, educators, peers, and the popular press.

SECTION I

The Pressure to Go to College
From Parents and Others

The go-to-college message in today's society is everywhere. Faith in the axiom that college is good has converted nearly everyone. According to one Gallup Poll (Gray, 1993), 93% of respondents said college was important to individual future success. The reinforcement to the go-to-college message pops up when one least expects it. Even our local automatic teller machine greets patrons with the question, "Need money for college?"; it hints of possible profits from college mania.

The pressure on high school seniors to continue their education is intense and relentless. It takes a lot of courage not to go to a 4-year college, especially if one is academically blessed. Perhaps the best evidence lies in the sheer number of students who want to go on to higher education. Anyone who has ever worked with high school students knows that the likelihood of getting 95% to agree on anything, even pizza and rock and roll, is about as likely as successfully herding cats. Thus, when 95% of graduating seniors say they plan to go on to higher education, and nationally almost 70% actually do, the intensity and effectiveness of the press to go to college can be appreciated. This pressure is applied in the form of well-intentioned advice first from parents.

Pressure From Parents

Although most teens who go to college will say they made the decision themselves, their decision was not made in a vacuum. Parents seem to be the important group influencing them. For example, Hossler and Stage (1992) found that parents' expectations were the single best predictor of going to college; this was particularly true in low-income homes. Although parents may have little influence on fashions, choice of music, or friends, when it comes to the decision about going to college, they call the shots.

If the importance given to parental advice is true, one would expect that, given the dramatic increase in college attendance, more parents are recommending college. NCES data confirm this hypothe-

TABLE 2.1 Percentage Recommending College to High School
Age Students: 1980s and 1990s

	Father		Mother		Guidance Counselor		Teachers	
	1980s	1990s	1980s	1990s	1980s	1990s	1980s	1990s
Total	59.1	77.0	64.8	82.9	32.3	65.2	32.3	65.5
Male	55.6	74.0	61.6	80.7	32.2	64.0	32.1	64.2
Female	63.5	80.0	68.6	85.2	32.7	66.3	32.5	66.8
Test Quartile								
Lowest	40.4	59.9	47.6	64.7	26.1	56.4	28.2	57.2
Second	49.7	71.7	55.6	79.3	26.1	61.1	26.5	60.7
Third	63.9	83.1	69.2	89.7	31.3	66.4	30.1	65.5
Highest	79.8	90.6	85.1	95.9	43.1	74.3	41.7	75.3

SOURCES: Compiled from *High School and Base Year Student Survey*, by the National Center for Education Statistics, 1982, Washington, DC: U.S. Department of Education; and *National Educational Longitudinal Study of 1988, 1992 Second Follow-Up*, by the National Center for Education Statistics, 1992, Washington, DC: U.S. Department of Education.

sis (see Table 2.1). Comparing the 1980s with the 1990s, the go-to-college message from parents increased 15% to 20%. In the 1990s, 85.2% of young women reported that their mothers had recommended college, as compared with 68.6% in the 1980s. It is also worth noting that, for both genders, mothers are stronger supporters of the go-to-college movement than fathers.

The focus of this book is students from the academic middle. Thus, we are interested in the extent and growth of parental pressure on high school graduates from the middle two quartiles. The growth in the percentage of parents recommending college actually increased fastest among students with the least academic ability. Cases in point are students in the second to lowest quartile, the bottom of the academic middle. The percentage of students in this category who reported that their fathers had recommended college increased 22% in 10 years. Even among those in the lowest quartile,

59.9% reported that their fathers had recommended college, whereas 64.7% reported that their mothers had recommended college.

No doubt, parents of high school students from the academic middle have their children's best interests in mind when they recommend college. They believe in the validity of the *one way to win* paradigm. Our model suggests that this conversion to college mania stems from a number of economic issues and social values. Before turning to these issues, we note other sources that exert the college press on academically average students. One such source is the one major social institution they all attend: their local high school.

Pressure From High Schools

The second most powerful source of pressure to go to college comes from the high schools themselves. Despite rhetoric to the contrary, high school staff have always viewed preparing students for college as their most important mission. Typically, the community agrees. Today, the instructional effectiveness of high school and college attendance rates has become one and the same in the public eye. Although high school educators will point to the community for this "college-or-nothing" criterion for success, it is largely self-imposed and historical in nature. When high schools began to proliferate at the turn of the century, most high school educators saw themselves as saving students from the "dreaded influence of the shop floor." This attitude was so common that industrialists openly accused high school educators of discouraging students from entering the trades (Gray, 1980).

Having set themselves up to be judged by the number of students who go to college, it is not surprising that high school staffs themselves exert significant overt and covert pressure on students to go on to college. Some of this pressure is institutionalized. High schools, for example, sponsor all types of activities aimed at helping students decide to attend college: college fairs, campus visitations, financial aid and college choice workshops for parents, and hosting college recruiters. Similar services and efforts are not made for teens who wish to go directly to work.

In some cases, the institutional pressure exerted by high schools on students to go to college is not particularly subtle. At some high school graduations, for example, the program includes a list of graduates, the colleges they are planning to attend, and scholarships they have been awarded. Now that's pressure. How would you like to be a parent with no college listed after your child's name? How would the child feel?

Perhaps the most repugnant method of institutionalizing the *one way to win* message by high schools is the weighted grading policies that give extra value to grades earned in special college prep courses typically taken by the academically blessed. Thus, an A in accounting, a career-related course, counts less than an A in honors English, a college prep course. The message to the student body could not be more obvious: Value is placed on preparation for college; those who are valued here take these courses.

The go-to-college message that is pervasive in high schools also comes directly from the faculty. Among the "true believers" in *one way to win* are high school teachers and even some guidance counselors. Both should know better. Even the pecking order among high school faculty reflects the value placed on college. The teachers with the highest status teach only those preparing for college. According to disturbing research by Oakes (1985) and others, teachers in the average high school have a pejorative view of noncollege-bound teens. Apparently, Taylorism (Gray, 1993)—the belief that the wealth of the nation depends on the contributions of the academically blessed, whereas those from the middle and lower ends of the academic spectrum are relatively less important—is alive and well. This theme is explored in later chapters.

This bias in favor of the academically blessed—the college-bound—elite is not new; thus, it contributes little to explanations of the recent and dramatic increase in college attendance among students from the academic middle. What has changed is the extent of teachers' and counselors' enthusiasm for advising students to go to college. Again, of particular interest is the advice given to students in the lower three quartiles. The same pattern of advice observed among parents is found among teachers and counselors. The percentage of students in the lower three quartiles who reported that their counselor had recommended college doubled or tripled between the 1980s and 1990s (see Table 2.1). Thus, the go-to-college message heard by academically average teens at home is reinforced at their high schools. This point is rather perplexing because, if any group could be expected to realistically assess an individual student's ability to benefit from higher education, it would be high school teachers and counselors. These individuals appear to have assessed the politics and decided instead to look the other way. This situation is discussed in Chapter 4. Of course, parents and teachers are not the only important influences on today's youth. Media and friends also deliver the message that "there is only *one way to win*—you had better go to college."

Pressure From Peers
and the Media

The influence of peer pressure on adolescent behavior is legendary. Especially as graduation approaches, all conversation among teens eventually turns to one question: "What are you going to do next year?" It is the rare teenager who is willing to say anything but, "I am going to college."

Added to the go-to-college din from parents, teachers, counselors, and friends is a constant barrage of *one way to win* propaganda in the public media. The press constantly reminds youth that 4-year college grads earn more. Often what is written is misleading. For example, in the late '90s, a headline in the press reported that the job outlook for 4-year college grads was never better. A closer reading, however, reveals that the outlook for those with specialized skills related to information technology was never better; the prospect for those with degrees in soft-skill college majors—which was and still is the majority—was terrible. Only recently has the press even hinted at the growing underemployment of university grads.

Equally important, the popular press plays an important role in the delivery of the go-to-college message from politicians. Even presidential campaign rhetoric promotes "go to college." When presidential candidates state, "All who want to go to college should be able to," the message is all too often interpreted as meaning that those who do not wish to are deficient in some way.

The go-to-college message from parents, teachers, and friends is nothing new. What is new is its persuasiveness and the fact that it is now delivered to all students regardless of academic ability. This change in attitude toward the appropriateness of "college for everyone" can be traced first to increased anxiety about the economic future of the nation and to conventional wisdom that developed about future career opportunities. Second, it can be attributed to several deep-seated cultural values about equal opportunity and the right to fail.

SECTION II

The Economic and Social Forces Behind *One Way to Win*

The pressure on teens to pursue the *one way to win* strategy comes from parents, teachers, peers, and the media, who in turn, preach the philosophy because they believe it. Understanding the biases of this belief is important for those who wish to suggest *other ways to win.*

Three variables are discussed here: economic uncertainty, the relationship of education and status, and the ideology of equal opportunity. Each of these variables leads to a predilection to support the *one way to win* mentality. We begin with an examination of the role of economic uncertainty.

Diminishing Economic Opportunities

The fact that the growth in the percentage of students entering higher education began about the same time as the massive economic restructuring in this country is more than a coincidence. One result of this restructuring was the permanent loss of many high-wage, low-skill jobs. As a result, the earnings of all except college graduates began to slip. The majority of today's youth and their parents, and perhaps almost everyone else, really are not sure where good work, both rewarding and high paying, will be found in the future. The only thing that now seems certain is the mathematical fact that those with a college degree, on average, earn more than those without one. This well-publicized fact, coupled with murky information about the rise of technical work, has led to several wide-spread labor market beliefs or assumptions that are mostly myths.

Labor Market Misconceptions

The *one way to win* or college mania mentality has been fueled by misinformation or myths about the future world of work. Five such misconceptions seem to underlie much of the rhetoric behind the *one way to win* mentality:

Labor market myths:

1. In the future, most jobs will require a 4-year college degree.
2. Most high-wage jobs in the future will be in technical fields that require a 4-year college degree.
3. Because 4-year college graduates earn more than those having less education, a 4-year degree guarantees above-average earnings.
4. The total labor force demand for college graduates is sufficient to ensure commensurate employment for all that receive a 4-year college degree.
5. In light of the oversupply of 4-year college graduates, college graduates will displace nondegree holders in good jobs that do not require a college degree.

As will be discussed in detail in Chapter 7, all five of these labor market beliefs are false, particularly for most of the academic middle. It is this group that enter 4-year colleges—despite mediocre to poor academic skills—that are the least likely to graduate in the first place. But if they do, they are also the least likely to find commensurate employment. They would be better off considering other ways to win, such as postsecondary prebaccalaureate technical education and other routes to high skill/high wage employment.

The sobering reality is that only 24% of all work in the future will require any postsecondary education: Almost half of all work requires less than 2 weeks' on-the-job training. And although the fastest-growing type of high skill/high wage employment is in technical areas, most employment will be at the technician level; only about 25% of technical jobs will require a 4-year degree or higher.

The True Concern
of Teens and Parents

The most important of the widely held economic misconceptions that fuel the *one way to win* mentality are the last two on the list—important because they are the primary rationales for most teens and parents.

Though precious few teens have taken the time to think about their career plans—even though getting a good job is why they enroll—most have this faith that there will be ample employment for 4-year college graduates. Thus, all they have to do is get a degree in something and everything will work out. Unfortunately their faith or optimism is unfounded. As will be discussed in Chapter 7, statistics from the federal departments of Education and Labor demonstrate clearly that there will be only about half as many jobs for 4-year college graduates as are needed to accommodate them. The number to remember is 57. That is the predicted number of jobs requiring a 4-year degree for every 100 that earn one. This means that 43 will go underemployed, taking jobs that do not require a 4-year degree. Importantly, this is just a year-by-year number and does not take into account that each year the underemployed from previous years are still looking. Thus, the true labor market outlook for 4-year college graduates is actually worse.

Some teens and many parents sense this reality. At work, parents have seen college-level jobs vanish due to downsizing and many have acquaintances whose children have graduated only to move back home. The chief concern behind the *one way to win* mentality is that, *as the number of those who hold a 4-year degree grows, a baccalaureate degree will be needed to compete for any type of decent employment.* Of course, there is some truth to this belief. Rumors abound that supposed low-level jobs now require a 4-year degree. One of the more popular is the one about the want ad for a warehouse job that requires a BA and ability to lift 30 lbs. Though probably not true, tales such as these are becoming more and more common and do not go unnoticed by teens and parents. To some extent, their fears are justified. Today, most bank clerks and many telemarketers—not to mention truck drivers—hold university degrees.

There is an important counterpoint to be made, however. Whereas it is certain that 4-year college graduates will be forced to take jobs that do not require the degree, they will be primarily in low-skill or soft-skill, low-wage occupations. It must be emphasized that *university graduates will not take jobs away from those with specific job skills in demand: In particular, those with 4-year degrees in soft-skill areas will not displace technicians educated at the prebaccalaureate level.* This latter point is critical for teens, parents, and those who would promote *other ways to win* to understand. In the future, academic degrees will become less and less important. More and more important will be technical skills. Thus, many information technology firms care little about a person's degrees but are very concerned about what technology certificates he or she holds. As will be stressed again and again in this book, the secret to *other ways to win* is the acquiring of job skills necessary to compete for high skill/ high wage employment.

The importance of misconceptions and fears regarding economic security as the root cause of the *one way to win* mentality cannot be overstated. Economic uncertainty about future labor market opportunities alone, however, does not adequately explain the go-to-college press that existed to a lesser extent even during the post-World War II economic golden years. Other forces at work center on social status and a prejudice toward nonprofessional work, as well as on deep-seated cultural values.

Social Class and Status

Even before the onset of economic uncertainty, the push to go to college was still very strong. Obviously, something other than economic uncertainty is at work. One such factor in the United States—inherited from our English forebears—is the relationship between social class and/or status and college attendance. Academicians are fond of portraying the benefits of higher education in terms of a more fulfilling and rewarding life. In reality, however, long before college had anything to do with careers other than medicine, law, or the clergy, higher education was popular for an entirely different reason: It was a vestige of social class and status. As the British aristocracy grew, the number of titles that could be bestowed by the monarch did not. A new vestige was needed—something less vulgar than just money—and college was ideal. Because at first few could afford to attend college, it was the perfect status symbol separating "gentle-

TABLE 2.2 Occupation Classification by Level

Classification	Occupation
1. Professional managerial (higher)	Doctor, lawyer, professor
2. Professional managerial (lower)	Teacher, engineer
3. Semiprofessional and management	Librarian, nurse, photographer
4. Skilled	Medical lab technician, machinist
5. Semiskilled	Firefighter, truck driver
6. Unskilled	Laborer

SOURCE: From "A New classification of Occupations," by A. Roe; 1954, *Journal of Counseling Psychology, 3.* Copyright by American Psychological Association; used with permission.

men" from the masses. This value was brought to the United States and is still alive and well. Even though higher education is very accessible, having a college degree is equated with the middle and upper classes. Thus, the relationship between social class, status, and college is a strong force behind the go-to-college message. This force is a particularly powerful reason for parental advice to go to college (more about this in Chapter 4). One related aspect of the correlation among social class identity, status, and college is a less overt but no less powerful prejudice against "dirty," blue-collar, nonprofessional work.

The Prejudice Against Nonprofessional Work

Although the public may support the platitude that there is dignity in all work, the only work given much status is professional work. "My daughter, the doctor" or "my son, the lawyer," is still the standard against which all else is compared. Evidence for this point of view could fill several books, but, for the sake of brevity, let's examine a standard occupational listing that ranks occupational fields according to the status that American society assigns to each (see Table 2.2).

It is not surprising to find professionals at the top and unskilled labor at the bottom. The middle rankings, however, are the interesting ones. Notice that skilled occupations are listed below semi-professional occupations despite the fact that most skilled occupations pay higher wages than most semiprofessional jobs—higher even than some professional occupations. Skilled precision workers continue to have higher average earnings than schoolteachers, so why are colleges full of students preparing to be teachers when there are jobs for only a fraction of them? Why is hardly anyone preparing for careers in the crafts? The reason is related to status. Teachers may not have the status of a doctor, a lawyer, or even an accountant, but they have more status than a precision metal worker who earns considerably more than they do.

This message is conveyed to youth: White- or striped-collar jobs are valued; all others are not. Furthermore, the belief is that those who do nonprofessional work are not very bright and are ill-mannered and generally unsophisticated. These stereotypes are reinforced in the media by the likes of Al Bundy and Homer Simpson, the so-called Joe Six-Packs. Aside from social class and status, several other deep-seated cultural values create a fertile climate for the *one way to win* mentality. Chief among them is the importance given in the United States to ensuring "equal opportunity" and the related belief in the "right to fail."

The Ideology of Equal Opportunity

The United States of America is frequently referred to as the land of opportunity. Such platitudes reflect a basic value in U.S. culture that affects the public's thinking about many things, including higher education. This basic value also creates a climate for acceptance of the *one way to win* mentality. In a nation where almost everyone's ancestors came from somewhere else. Except for those who were forced to come here in slavery, the rest came here for the promise of a better life, keeping open avenues or opportunities for a better life for the nation's youth has strong support. The population in general and educators in particular have traditionally discouraged youth from making career decisions too early, thinking that it could limit future opportunity. This view is one basis of the belief that as many students as possible should be sent to college. In recent times, opportunity and college have come to be viewed as one and the same. College recruiters know this and play on it heavily. Marketing slogans such as "Imagine the impossible, then do it" and "This fall is not too late to turn your life around" (both gleaned from the *New York Times*) are typical plays on the doctrine of equal opportunity. This doctrine not only promotes college mania but also makes the topics of rising costs, lack of ability, inadequate preparation for college, and lack of career direction difficult to deal with, even though it is obvious that encouraging everyone to go to college while ignoring these factors may not be such a good idea. This is especially true since college has come to be viewed as the great provider of equal opportunity.

As suggested more than 25 years ago by the eminent sociologist Burton Clark (1962), a consistent problem in democracies is that although the culture encourages aspirations, it is ineffective in providing equal opportunity to achieve them. This dilemma, argues Clark, is a strong motivator behind the conventional wisdom he calls the "ideology of equal opportunity." It argues that society should provide unlimited access to higher education. As Clark points out, "Strictly interpreted, equality of opportunity means selection [to college] according to ability, without regard to extraneous considerations. Popularly interpreted, however, equal opportunity in obtaining a college education is widely taken to mean 'unlimited access' " (p. 580).

This ideology of equal opportunity is a strong force behind the *one way to win* mentality. Even suggesting that unlimited access to higher education may not be in the interests of either the nation or its citizens puts one at risk of being politically incorrect. This fear may be one reason that few question college mania. Instead of confronting the problem, society has chosen what Clark refers to as the "soft response": Funds are provided to ensure unlimited access and thus allow a sort of higher education Darwinism to take place as half slowly drop out or, as Clark suggests, "cool out." Of course, the irony is that those who cool out are those whom the doctrine of opportunity was supposed to help the most; instead, they are most likely to fail. It is difficult to understand how they are supposed to benefit from the experience (this reality is discussed in Chapter 3). Even raising these questions is problematic because of the second deep-seated belief about youth—that they have the right to try and the right to fail.

In most countries, the idea of supporting the attendance of large numbers of youth in college who do not have the academic ability and/or preparation to be successful would be unimaginable, and dropout rates of 50% would be intolerable. But this belief is not shared in the United States, at least not yet. Why? First, because we are perhaps the only nation that can afford these social inefficiencies. Second, this situation is tolerated because of a basic value that career development specialist Ken Hoyt (1994) calls the "right to try" and the "right to fail." That "1 in 100" individual who "battles the odds" and succeeds despite a poor high school record seems always to be in the back of the minds of Americans. Because of such outside possibilities of success, the nation has been willing to let the Darwinian "cooling out" process in higher education take its course. Of course, to do so, two final enabling ingredients are needed: open college admissions and student financial aid.

SECTION III

The Enablers Behind *One Way to Win:* Open Admissions and Financial Aid

In this chapter, we have discussed the various groups that deliver the *one way to win*—go-to-college—message and the economic fears, misconceptions, ideologies, and values that lead them to do so. It is interesting to observe that, to varying degrees, these pressure groups, economic uncertainties, and social values exist in all other nations. The United States leads the world in the percentage of youth who go on to a 4-year college, partly because (a) it is the only place that totally disregards academic ability by allowing open admissions, (b) it awards financial aid on the basis of need—not academic ability, and (c) it disregards the fact that only one in four who begin a 4-year degree program graduates and/or finds commensurate employment. In France, for example, 28% go on to college; in Great Britain, 13%; and in Germany, 20% (Hoyt, 1994). Why? Obviously, factors in the United States that enable graduating high school students to play the *one way to win* game regardless of academic ability do not exist abroad. Two enablers predominate: empty college seats and government-supported student financial aid.

Open College Admissions

As frequently as college faculties deny it, higher education is a business in which the number of suppliers—colleges—continues to grow out of proportion to the number of traditional customers—graduating high school seniors. By way of illustration, between 1981 and 1991 the number of colleges and universities in the United States actually increased by 328, whereas the number of high school graduates decreased by 250,000 (NCES, 1992). According to Paul Fussell (1983), writer, social commentator, and a leading cynic about college mania, more institutions in the state of Ohio call themselves universities than there are in all of unified Germany.

This excess of college seats supercharges college mania in two ways. First, it removes the obstacle of admission standards; as enrollment declines, colleges take in fewer qualified applicants, finally all applicants. This situation led Albert Shanker to comment, in the quote at the beginning of this chapter, that everyone might as well be given a college degree at birth because academic ability and achievement in high school are no longer needed.

Second, it promotes the *one way to win* mentality in a subtler way. Declining enrollments have become the principal issue at most colleges. "Enrollment management" is a big issue in higher education. Make no mistake—the goal is to keep the classes and dorm rooms full.

Marketing efforts to fill empty college dorms and classes have become sophisticated and extensive. The most prevalent advertising tactic used in these campaigns is to play on the hopes and fears behind the *one way to win* mentality. The net result is that, in the effort to fill seats, higher education spends millions of dollars each semester promoting the go-to-college message. By doing so, it reinforces the *one way to win* mentality. Thus, aside from parents, high school faculty, and friends, colleges themselves are probably the biggest source of go-to-college rhetoric. The product they are promoting is expensive, but this is not a problem because the government is more than willing to pay.

Nonmerit Financial Aid

Because the doors to higher education are wide open, the only problem is obtaining the money to pay tuition bills. Even this is not quite the problem it could be, because of the availability of financial aid. As reported earlier, the majority of students in college now receive financial aid. Significantly, this aid is awarded, not on merit or on need and merit, but just on need. Thus, although in the distant past excellent academic credentials were needed to get a scholarship or grant, this is no longer true. Right or wrong, this need-based rather than merit-based philosophy of financial aid, coupled with excess higher education capacity, has put college within reach of marginally qualified students from the academic middle. We are not saying that costs are not a problem (they are an increasingly important issue with parents), but need-based financial aid softens the risks of going to college unprepared and is an important enabler of the *one way to win* mentality.

Other Ways to Win

In this chapter, we have explored the forces behind the *one way to win* mentality. National survey research suggests that the most direct reason for increased college attendance among seemingly unqualified students is a change in attitude among parents, teachers, and counselors about the need to go to college regardless of preparation. This change in attitude can be traced most directly to economic uncertainty and related myths about future labor market opportunities. These fears and the *one way to win* solution are then buttressed by deep-seated cultural values about class identification, the superiority of professional work, the perceived relationship between college and equal opportunity, and the right to choose and the right to fail.

The United States has created a form of higher education Darwinism that allows all to try. From admission onward, the emphasis is on survival of the fittest among students. The costs of this cooling out process were described in Chapter 1. It is particularly costly to those who need help the most, namely, those from the academic middle of the nation's graduating high school senior classes. The irony is that, in this group, youth from disadvantaged homes—and females in general—bear the brunt of the damage done by providing only *one way to win*. These groups would benefit most from the creation of *other ways to win*.

Note

1. As quoted in Mark Pitsch, 1994, p. 4. Copyright © 1994, *Education Week*. Reprinted by permission.

3

Limited Options for
Special Populations

Sometimes when people start out to do good, evil follows.
Daniel Patrick Moynihan[1]

I f the percentage of graduating high school seniors enrolling in 4-year colleges immediately after graduation is any
indication, the *one way to win* paradigm—the conventional wisdom that a baccalaureate degree and professional work are
the only ways to the American dream—has become a pervasive,
widely shared belief. A close look reveals that the largest group of recent high school graduates enrolled in 2-year colleges actually are
taking general studies programs designed to prepare them for transfer to a 4-year baccalaureate degree program. Although the validity
of the paradigm's advice is questionable, the real dilemma is the financial and personal costs to those who follow the advice. These
costs are measured in terms of decreased international economic
competitiveness, tuition dollars and student loans, and human failure, alienation, and unmet expectations. Although this harm takes
its toll on all youth—surprising numbers of the academically blessed
drop out during their freshman year—those students who comprise
the academic middle of the nation's high schools are disproportion-
ately harmed. Within this group, two subgroups—those from economically disadvantaged households and young women—are par-

ticularly vulnerable. These two subgroups are the focus of this chapter.

Our argument is that, although sincere, those promoting the pursuit of a 4-year degree and professional work as the end-all strategy for achieving equal opportunity for disadvantaged youth and closing the wage gap between men and women are also naively optimistic and ultimately harmful. Ironically, by advocating and valuing only one alternative, they may be doing more harm than good to many of those they seek to help the most. The youth in these two subgroups are the most likely to be hurt by indiscriminantly advising the academic middle to go to a 4-year college in the hope of landing a job in the professional ranks.

SECTION I

Economically Disadvantaged Youth

Twenty percent of all children in the United States live in poverty. In any randomly assigned classroom in the country, one would find at least one third of the students living at or below 20% of the poverty level. In some states it is more than half, and in some rural and urban school districts it could be virtually all. Though progress was made in lowering the poverty rate in the late 1990s, the decrease was measured only in tenths of a percent. And, although the poverty rate for African Americans (26.5%) and Hispanics (27.1%) exceeds that of whites, the experience of all economically disadvantaged children is pretty much the same regardless of race. They enter elementary school at a disadvantage and face the same future. For example, black and white students who must repeat the first grade are just as likely to drop out of school (NCES, 1988).

Breaking the poverty cycle for disadvantaged youth, be they majority or minority, has proven to be a perplexing problem. In decades past, the great hope was increasing high school graduation rates. Today it is the *one way to win* paradigm. One national study found, for example, that among high school sophomores, a higher percentage of African Americans aspired to college than white students (NCES, 1988). And, of course, the *one way to win* message means the same for disadvantaged youth as it does for those from higher-income families: To get a better job in the professions, get a 4-year degree.

Is the indiscriminate urging of all disadvantaged youth to pursue the *one way to win* strategy a good idea? Just as with more advantaged teens, the answer lies in the results. Again, whereas the *one way to win* philosophy is certainly appropriate for some disadvantaged youth and it ensures that they can pursue a matter of national pride, the question remains: Is it good advice for all? Logic alone suggests otherwise. But there are more specific concerns.

In his book, *Street Wise,* Elijah Anderson (1990) argues that, among urban youth, the best predictor of persistence and success in school is hope for a better future. At the same time, according to other researchers, although low-income youth may have the same ambitions as their more blessed peers, their expectations for achieving these goals are significantly less. Thus, although hope is critical to breaking the poverty cycle, telling economically disadvantaged youth that their only hope is a bachelor's degree is counterproductive. For many, a 4-year college degree is beyond their perception of the possible. As a result, they end up with no hope. Some drop out for a life on the streets or dead-end jobs; others find it safer and socially acceptable to stay in school with their friends. The latter group come to school each day but tune out when in class. These youth deserve better. Holding out only one valued alternative—a 4-year college degree—is cruel and unethical and does them more harm than good. For one thing, they are the least likely to be academically ready for such a challenge.

One problem with advocating the *one way to win* strategy for all economically disadvantaged youth is that, as a group, they are the least likely to be academically prepared. While socially unacceptable, the reality is that the likelihood of being prepared to do 4-year college academics is directly correlated with family household income. For example, 53% of 1992 low-income (less than $25,000) high school graduates have sufficient academic qualifications for admission to a 4-year college, compared with 68% of middle-income ($25,000–$74,999) graduates and 86% of graduates from high-income families (NCES, 1998, Indicator 8).

The unavoidable fact is that low-income students are the least prepared for a university education. As a result, high percentages of those students who try the *one way to win* strategy end up taking remedial courses in college. These courses cost the same but do not count toward a degree. Although justified on the grounds of providing opportunity or a second chance for these students, the problem is that they are largely ineffective at doing so: Most who take these courses never graduate.

The plight of economically disadvantaged youth from the academic middle who pursue the *one way to win* paradigm is about the same as more advantaged teens from the middle—the majority of both groups fail to graduate—but there is one important difference that seems to be totally disregarded. For teens from low-income families, the consequences of trying the *one way to win* path and then failing are a lot worse. Why? Because those from middle- and upper-income families are (a) much less likely to have student loan debt and (b) if they do, they are more likely to have financial help from their families. Thus, while the *one way to win* mantra is not benign for all youth, it can be particularly devastating for those from low-income families who fail.

Now we ask, Does this grim picture mean that low-income youth should be discouraged from 4-year higher education? Of course not. Although some will argue that everyone should have an equal right to fail, we argue that until society can ensure equal probabilities of success and equal costs of failure for all youth, indiscriminately promoting a 4-year college education to low-income youth from the academic middle of the nation's high schools sets up too many for failure. Such a situation could, in fact, be construed as a conspiracy to ensure their failure. Youth from economically disadvantaged homes desperately need hope, alternatives, and *other ways to win*.

The good news is that, arguably, economically disadvantaged youth have the most to gain from considering *other ways to win*. Why? Because they are generally dramatically underrepresented in the second- and third-highest paying occupational group, namely crafts, precision manufacturing, specialized repair, and technical support (see Table 3.1). This is particularly true for women, but it is also the case for African Americans and Hispanics. Their share of jobs in these occupational groups should be similar to their percentage of the total labor force, specifically, women (46.2%), African Americans (10.8%), and Hispanics (9.8%). Obviously, this is not the case; all three groups are underrepresented. As a result, many employers are actively seeking women and people of color. Most occupations in these two groups do not require a 4-year degree; in some cases, no degree at all. They all require significant training, as verified by completing a high school vocational program, coupled with a 1- or 2-year postsecondary prebaccalaureate technical education, a formal apprenticeship program, or relevant military service.

SECTION II

Women and the Gender Wage Gap

Among the true believers in the *one way to win* philosophy, young women appear to be the most zealous. In 1999, there were 2 million more women in higher education than men. They earned 57% of all bachelor's degrees. The female/male higher education enrollment ratio has become so lopsided that some 4-year colleges are now actively recruiting males. Like their male counterparts, women are in college primarily to "get a better job" (see Table 1.1). In some studies, young women are actually more apt than young men to say that "being successful in work" and "being able to find steady work" are "very important" to them.

Again we ask, Is this development good or bad? Again, the results suggest that celebrations may be premature. Overall, the prognosis for young women from the academic middle that pursue the *one way to win* strategy is about the same as for young men; they enroll in third- or fourth-tier institutions, take remedial courses, only slightly higher percentages graduate, and their prospects are few when they do graduate. As an indication, despite rising educational levels, women are still twice as likely as men to be at high risk of underemployment and eight times as likely to be at medium risk of underemployment as men (Mohammed, 1998). One reason for high underemployment is the choices women make in college. Women are five to eight times more likely to choose majors related to the helping professions than those in engineering, management, computer science, or nonprofessional technical areas such as drafting, construction, or manufacturing (American Council on Education, 1999). Importantly, virtually all the technical majors that lead to high skill/high wage employment are dominated by men.

Women still cluster in low-paying professional occupations. A recent population survey conducted by the federal government found that only 28% of computer systems analysts and 31% of computer programmers were women, even though 70% or more of these workers were younger than 44 (U.S. Department of Commerce, 1998). Young women are three to four times less likely than men to major in electrical engineering or computer science and six times less likely to major in 2-year associate-degree technical programs.

One of the reasons so many young women try the *one way to win* game is that they seem not to know of *other ways to win*. It is worth noting, for example, that among entering college freshman, women are 25% more likely than men to be undecided about careers. When pressed to make a choice, they all make the same choice: 68% hope to land a job in the professions.

Meanwhile, some researchers who seek to narrow the gender wage gap have concluded that the problem is no longer too few women executives, but too few women in other high skill/high wage occupations. Thus, Terrell (1992) argues that narrowing the wage gap in the future will depend on breaking up sex segregation among occupations. Although some of the unequal representation of women in high-paying professional occupations may still have to do with gender barriers, or "glass ceilings," in the case of many other high-paying occupations, one major reason is that few women aspire to, and thus do not prepare for, these careers.

The problem is that, although women are gaining parity in the professions, they are seriously underrepresented in high-paying nonprofessional careers. Table 3.1 lists the six occupational groups (used often in this book) identified by the U.S. Bureau of the Census. In the table, the occupational groups are not listed alphabetically, but rather from highest to lowest according to the average yearly income of those who work in each group. The table reports the percentage of women employed in each occupational group. The message is clear: Although women have nearly gained parity (47%) in the highest-paid managerial and professional group, they represent only 9% of the labor force in the second highest-paid group—crafts, precision metal, and specialized repair. Furthermore, although women reportedly comprise 64% of technical support workers, this category includes clerical workers and so is misleading. A look at other nonclerical technical support occupations also reveals that women are very underrepresented.

Breaking down the barriers to occupations that do not traditionally include women will be the real feminist challenge in the future. Telling all women that they should go to college in the hope of

TABLE 3.1 Percentage of Labor Force and Occupational Groups Comprising Women, African Americans, and Hispanics

	Women	African American	Hispanic
Total labor force	46	11	10
Managerial/professional	49	7	5
Precision manufacturing/ crafts/ special repair	9	8	12
Technical support (includes clerical)	64	10	8
Service	60	16	15
Operators/laborers	25	7	15
Farming	19	1	20

SOURCE: U.S. Dept of Labor. Bureau of Labor Statistics (1998, January). http://stats.bls.gov/cpsaatab.htm

entering the professional ranks—the *one way to win* message—is counterproductive. History has already proven that too many women take this advice, only to end up employed in clerical positions because they could not obtain a teaching job or get into law school. Meanwhile, the demand for women in high skill/high wage occupations that require only a prebaccalaureate postsecondary education is staggering. Yet, the typical profile of a woman who begins a career in a nontraditional occupational area for women is 32 years old, is divorced, and has children (Sternberg and Tuchscherer, 1992). Young women are six times less likely than men to major in 2-year associate degree technical programs (American Council on Education, 1999). Obviously, young women currently are seeing only *one way to win*. Those who seek to improve their plight in the labor market would do well to help them consider *other ways to win*.

Other Ways to Win

One major way the *one way to win* mentality is promoted is from the well-intended efforts of government, advocacy groups, and individuals who hope that a 4-year college education will break the poverty cycle and improve the earnings of females relative to males. Unfortunately, the pursuit of a 4-year college degree in preparation for a professional career is an appropriate strategy for only some low-income youth and some women; it is not realistic for all, particularly for those from the academic middle. First, many impoverished youth view college as an impossible wannabe dream, and without alternatives, they lose hope and give up. But among the impoverished youth who do not give up and do enter college, those from the academic middle are, on average, the least prepared to be successful, the most likely to have to take remedial course work, the most likely to drop out or cool out, and the least able to cope with the financial consequences. Likewise, some argue that the *one way to win* mentality is leading a majority of young females from the academic middle of high school seniors down a labor market path to professions that are too narrow to accommodate them. Meanwhile, other more promising career paths for women go untraveled.

Of course, these arguments demand proof that (a) those in the academic middle are unprepared to do college-level work, (b) when they go to college they do not do well, and (c) those who do graduate will face a very overcrowded labor market for 4-year college graduates. We provide this evidence and discuss the reasons for the public's blind eye toward this travesty in Part 2 of this book. Our discussion begins in Chapter 4 with an honest look at the high school academic preparation of students who make up the academic middle.

Note

1. Daniel Patrick Moynihan, 1994, August 7. *The New York Times Magazine*, p. 26. Copyright © 1994 by The New York Times Company. Reprinted by permission.

II

Counting the Losers in the *One Way to Win* Game

4

Questionable
Academic Preparation

The message that flows out to American high school kids is that it makes absolutely no difference how well you do [in high school] because it doesn't matter.

M. Tucker (1994, p. 7)[1]

At one time, going to college was unusual; today, the high school graduate who goes directly to work is the oddity. By the end of the 1990s, on average, 1.8 million high school graduates enrolled immediately in higher education, whereas less than 20% of all graduates went to work or entered the military. Of those in higher education, two thirds enrolled in 4-year colleges, and at least one third of those who enrolled in 2-year institutions are not taking occupational programs but general studies courses. Thus, of all high school graduates, the vast majority go to college and the largest group enroll in 4-year colleges or 2-year programs in preparation for transfer to a baccalaureate degree program. Is this a positive development? Perhaps not, if many are academically unprepared to benefit from the experience. Thus, it seems prudent to ask this question: How many of these 1.8 million new college freshmen are prepared to do college work? Our focus of analysis is the effectiveness of the revered and respected high school college prep curriculum.

SECTION I

How Effective Is the
College Prep Program of Study?

Today most youth aspire to baccalaureate education. Not surprisingly, the majority also say they took the college prep program in high school in order to prepare. But how many actually graduate prepared? Everyone? If not, then maybe the *one way to win* strategy is ill-advised for some.

If grades in high school are any indication, the college prep program is very effective. Throughout the 1990s, the reported average grade point average of entering college freshman increased. Ninety percent of the entering freshman in 1998 reported a B average or better; 32% had an A average (American Council on Education, 1999). Yet there is room for skepticism: During the same period, the number taking college remedial education and the college dropout rate also reached all-time highs. Perhaps a closer look is called for.

The first clue that all who say they are in the college prep program are not graduating prepared is to look at how many are really college prep students based on an examination of their high school transcripts. National data suggest that only 43% of students have completed a college prep program of study. More revealing, only 11% of students completed a vocational education program of study. *Thus, the largest group of students in high school are really in the general curriculum, meaning that they graduate neither prepared for college nor for full-time employment.*

Most students from the academic middle no longer concentrate in vocational/technical education programs, such as business education, vocational agriculture, or the building trades. But it is incorrect to assume that they are becoming legitimate college prep students. NCES data suggest that today this cohort is, in fact, general education students, taking some but not all the college prep courses. These students, and especially their parents, may think they are in the college prep program. But which one?

Part of the subterfuge caused by the growth of the *one way to win* mentality and the corresponding growth in the number of students wishing to take college prep courses has been the bifurcation of the college prep curriculum to distinguish between the academically blessed and those from the academic middle. Today, in virtually all

U.S. high schools, at least two college prep programs are going on si-
multaneously: One consists of the regular college prep courses; the
other is the college "honors" or "advanced placement" (AP) courses.
Most would consider the latter to be the college prep program of old.

The mere existence of these two levels of college prep programs
hints that one group of students may not be getting quite the same
preparation as the other. Surprisingly, no one seems concerned
about, or at least has questioned, the effectiveness of an unreformed
college prep curriculum that would serve all. Yet, what if the percentage of those who graduate with credentials (the predictor of success
in college) declines as enrollment increases? This trend would indicate a possible problem. It may be appropriate, then, to take a closer
look at the effectiveness of a college prep program of study in the
light of the large number of academically average students enrolling
in it.

The College Prep Program and
the Academically Average

Increases in enrollments in college prep programs have only recently resulted in investigations about its effectiveness for the academically diverse cohort participating in it. Specifically, if the objective of the college prep program is to prepare students for college
admission and success in college-level academic work, how many of
those who enroll actually achieve these outcomes? No doubt some
do, particularly if the academically blessed are separated into honors
classes with the best teachers. But what about the rest? This question
is important for those who suspect that the *one way to win* paradigm
may, in fact, encourage many academically average teens to pursue
postsecondary plans that are unrealistic and doomed to failure.

Several national studies suggest that if 72% of recent high school
graduates are in college within 2 years of graduating, two thirds of
whom are supposedly working toward a university degree, then
many are academically ill-prepared. One indicator is the National Assessment of Education Progress (NAEP) (National Center for Education Statistics, 1998) data for 17-year-olds (high school seniors). Table
4.1 indicates the percentage that scored at Levels 300 and 350 in reading and mathematics, respectively. Level 300 in reading is defined as
being able to understand complicated written information; Level 350

TABLE 4.1 National Assessment of Educational Progress:
              Percentage of 1997 High School Seniors Scoring at
              College Levels of Proficiency

Subject	Percentage
Reading	
Level 300: Understand complicated information	39
Level 350: Learn from specialized reading	6
Math	
Level 300: Moderately complicated procedure	60
Level 350: Multiple-step problem and algebra	7

SOURCE: National Center for Education Statistics, 1998.

is the ability to learn from specialized reading materials (such as college reading lists). Most would agree that wannabee college freshmen should be able to read at these levels, yet only 39% can read at Level 300 and 6% at Level 350. Level 350 in mathematics is the ability to solve mathematics problems using algebra; only 7% had mathematics skill at this level. Not very impressive.

   Equally interesting is a study done by the National Center for Educational Statistics (National Center for Education Statistics, 1998, Indicator 8) that sought to determine the percentage of youth who graduated from high school qualified to do college-level academics. Importantly, this study included only students who were already enrolled in 4-year colleges. The criteria included high school class rank, courses taken, and standardized test scores. For example, minimally qualified students need only to have to graduated in the top 50% of their high school class, have a C average, and have a combined SAT score of 820/composite ACT = 19. Table 4.2 shows the results.

   Table 4.2 suggests that, of all those in 4-year colleges, only two thirds are even minimally qualified. If one argues, as we do, that the minimally qualified are really not academically qualified to succeed in college, the result is rather sobering. *More than half (52%) of students pursuing the* one way to win *dream at 4-year colleges are not aca-*

TABLE 4.2 Percentage Distribution of 1992 High School
Graduates Qualified for Admission at a 4-Year
Institution, by Race/Ethnicity and Family Income,
1992-1994

Race/Ethnicity and Family Income	Marginally Qualified or Unqualified	College Qualified				
		Total	Minimally	Moderately	Highly	Very Highly
Total	35.5	64.5	16.6	15.9	18.2	13.8
Race/ethnicity						
White	31.9	68.2	16.1	16.6	20.3	15.2
Black	53.1	46.9	16.7	14.0	9.9	6.3
Hispanic	47.0	53.0	20.7	13.6	10.8	7.9
Asian/ Pacific islander	27.3	72.7	14.6	15.0	20.2	23.0
American Indian/ Alaskan native	55.2	44.8	22.2	15.8	5.9	1.0
Family income						
Low (less than $25,000)	47.5	52.5	18.7	12.8	13.6	7.3
Middle ($25,000-74,999)	32.4	67.6	16.1	17.0	19.9	14.6
High ($75,000 or more)	14.1	85.9	11.5	18.4	27.0	29.0

SOURCE: The National Center for Education Statistics, 1998

demically prepared. But if we were to take the old-fashioned view that
only highly qualified students should be pursuing a 4-year degree,
then the unavoidable summation is that only 32% are qualified to do

so. Little wonder that in some institutions, two thirds of entering freshman are in remedial education. Little wonder that 6 years later, only about half have graduated.

Additional insight into just how many so-called college prep students graduate from high school prepared to do college-level academics is supplied by research done by Gray and Xiaoli (1999). This study examined in detail the experiences of 1998 high school graduates.

The Class of 1998 Follow-Up Study

The best indicator of the need for promoting *other ways to win* at any particular high school is to look at what happens to its students the first year after graduation. However, unless it is based on what courses they took in high school, such evaluation is meaningless. For example, the implication of large numbers of students taking remedial courses in college depends clearly on what they did or did not take in high school. If most were quasi general/academic students, then it is understandable. If, on the other hand, many were in honors courses, the implications are quite different. Thus, rather than just sending graduates a questionnaire regarding their first-year experiences, a better approach is to also collect information regarding courses taken, grade point averages, absences, test scores, and so forth, for each graduate. This information is then used to develop a longitudinal data set that links students' high school records with their post-high school experiences (for more details, see Web site http://www.personal.psu.edu/faculty/g/t/gty/sld001.htm). This was the approach taken in the Follow-Up Study of the Class of 1998 (Gray & Xiaoli, 1998).

Seven high schools, selected to include inner-city urban, rural, and suburban locals, participated in the study. Regardless of the demographics, sending as many teens on to college as possible was the criterion of success. None of these high schools had an official general track program, and typically less than 15% of the students completed a concentration in vocational education. Thus, by default, most students must be considered to be in the academic–college prep program of study. The question we are asking is, How many were actually prepared? Unlike the NCES study (see Table 4.2) that evalu-

TABLE 4.3 Percentage of High School Graduates Prepared to Do College Level Academics

	Range of			
A: Prepared	*B: Marginally Prepared*	*A+B*	*C: Unprepared*	
10-27	18-28	28-55	45-72	
	Criterion			
3 Years College Prep Math	*2 Years College Lab Science*	*2 Years Same Foreign Language*	*Combined SAT Scores*	*High School GPA*

	3 Years College Prep Math	*2 Years College Lab Science*	*2 Years Same Foreign Language*	*Combined SAT Scores*	*High School GPA*
Prepared	Yes	Yes	Yes	≥1100	≥B
Marginal	Yes	Yes	Yes	≥800	≥C
Unprepared			Default		

SOURCE: Gray, K., & Xiaoli, S. (1999).

ated just those enrolled in 4-year colleges, this study looked at all 1998 high school graduates in the participating high schools.

Table 4.3 indicates the range of students at various high schools assigned to three levels of preparedness to do college level academics, namely, prepared, marginally prepared, and unprepared. The criteria used were 3 years of college math and two lab sciences, 2 years of the same foreign language, cumulative grade point averages, and combined Scholastic Aptitude Test (SAT) scores. Because of wide differences in demographic/socioeconomic settings of the participating high schools, ranges are provided instead of averages.

In order to be assigned to the academically prepared group, a student must have taken the required courses, earned a GPA of B or better, and have a combined (verbal + math) score of 1100. At the

TABLE 4.4 Post-High School Pursuits of Respondents (*1998 Follow-Up Study*)

Frequency Percentage Row Pct Col Pct	Full-time student	Full-time student working part time	Full-time employment	Part-time employment	Others
TOTAL	46	32	14	6	2
Prepared (acad. comp.)	71	27	1	1	0
Marginally prepared (semicomp.)	55	36	4	5	0
Unprepared (noncomp.)	23	33	29	10	5

SOURCE: *1998 Follow-Up Study* KCG/PSU

best-performing high schools, 27% of graduates had these credentials; at the other end, only 10% did. Of course, it can be argued that these criteria are too difficult. And it could also be argued that they are too lax; clearly they would not be sufficient to gain admission to colleges that still have competitive versus open admissions. Nonetheless, a second count was conducted to identify students who were marginally prepared, meaning that they probably could survive in college though some remediation might be necessary. Again, at the best-performing high school, these more lax standards added 28% versus 18% at the poorest-performing site. Perhaps most important is the column that combines these two levels: prepared and marginally prepared. In the best case, only 55% of the graduates were either prepared or marginally prepared. Yet, as will now be discussed, two thirds were in college anyway.

Going to College: Do Academic Credentials Matter?

From the information provided in Table 4.3, it is clear that, at best, about half of high school students graduate even semi-prepared to do college-level academics. Yet most were in college anyway. Not surprisingly, virtually all the prepared and semi-prepared graduates

Figure 4.1. Postsecondary Attendance: Academically Unprepared Noncompetitive Students: Class of 1991 Follow-Up Study

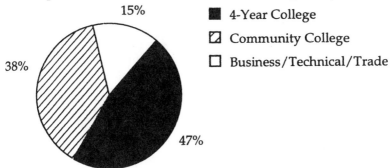

SOURCE: Gray, K., Wang, D., & Malizia, S. (1993).

were in college (see Table 4.4). But what about the group that interests us the most, those who graduate with credentials suggesting that they are not prepared to pursue the *one way to win* strategy? Amazingly, more than half were also in college. This finding is surprising for three reasons: None of these graduates (1) had a combined SAT score of over 800, (2) had taken a complete sequence of college prep courses, and (3) had maintained a C average. The expectation at this point may be that these students enroll mostly in 2-year institutions such as community colleges or technical schools. Apparently, however, the idea that it takes good academic credentials to get into a 4-year college is old-fashioned.

In general, the data support the *one way to win* paradigm: The only way to win is to have a 4-year college degree; 78% of all graduates were in 4-year colleges. What is startling, however, is that almost half (47%) of the students who graduated with academically noncompetitive credentials were also in 4-year colleges (see Figure 4.1). Of those in 2-year institutions, we can be only somewhat certain that the 15% in business and technical schools were not taking general studies courses in the hope of transferring to a 4-year degree program.

By looking at the analysis of high school transcripts discussed previously, the persuasiveness and results of the *one way to win* paradigm is illustrated. Consistent with national data, most students in this study were in the academic/college prep program of study. But, at best, only half graduated even marginally prepared to do college-level work and, of this group, about half had credentials that suggest college was going to be an academic stretch. Even though the other half (and in some high schools it is two thirds) are not prepared, at least half of this group are in college, and half are in 4-year colleges. How do they do in college? Also, we should not forget the students who went to work without having taken vocational education in high school. How do they make out in the world of work? We examine these questions in Chapter 5. But before turning to the postsecondary experiences of those in the academic middle, a closer look at the high school experiences of those who graduated with academically non-competitive credentials is worthwhile. After all, these are the students most likely to be hurt by the presence of only *one way to win.*

SECTION II

The High School Experience of Those in the Academic Middle

College Prep Course-Taking Patterns

How many math and science courses were taken by the academi-cally average students in this study? As part of the Class of 1998 Follow-Up Study (Gray & Xiaoli, 1999), data regarding levels of mathematics, science, and foreign language courses taken were collected from each student's transcript. After these patterns were summarized for just those who failed to earn either prepared marginally or semicompetitive prepared credentials, we found that the overall levels of math, science, and foreign languages taken by the remaining unprepared students were often quite high. Thus, one positive development of increasing percentages of all students in the college prep program is that, at least in these high schools, they did take higher levels of math and science than they would have if they had been in vocational education (for details regarding course-taking patterns for vocational education students, see U.S. Department of Education, 1994, pp. 112-113).

Yet, something seems odd, doesn't it? If these students had this much math and science, why did they do so poorly on the SAT? The data suggest that although these students were often enrolled in higher levels of math and science courses, they were somewhat untouched by the experience. Stated in another way, traditional college prep courses seem to be less effective for those in the academic middle. Unlike their more academically blessed peers, those in the academic middle may take a course but not master the content. This conclusion is substantiated by the low grades obtained by this group in these courses and by the fact that (as is reported in Chapter 5) half of those who graduated unprepared but went on to college had to take one or more remedial courses in higher education.

The point is that simply driving these students higher in the traditional curriculum—an oft-expressed goal among educational reformers—may not do much to improve their skills. Those who take solace in the fact that more academically average students are now in college prep courses are perhaps celebrating prematurely; students may be in the courses, but they may not be learning much. In fact, they often seem to be almost unaffected by the experience. This statement brings us to another important variable: the general degree of involvement of these students in the high school curriculum.

Involvement in the Curriculum

As researchers probe the results of the steady increase in the number of students who succeed in graduating from high school, it becomes increasingly apparent that completing high school and actually learning something are two entirely different things. This reality suggests that the goal is not only to keep young people in school—or even in class—but also to engage them as a prerequisite to learning (Anderson, 1983). Thus, those seeking to improve the instructional effectiveness of schools are increasingly focusing on students' degree of involvement in, or attachment to, the curriculum.

In the light of the growing body of literature suggesting the relationship between educational achievement and involvement—and common sense tells us that it is tough to learn by not paying attention—the researchers involved in the Class of 1998 Follow-Up Study employed statistical techniques to test the degree to which students were involved in the curriculum. They did this by testing the degree to which traditional variables, such as attendance, satisfaction with high school, and working part-time, affected students' grades. The rationale was that if the students were not very involved with learning in school, it would make little difference whether they were absent, liked school, or worked part-time. In fact, when compared with their more academically successful peers, the grades of those who graduated with academically noncompetitive credentials were relatively unaffected by the variables tested. Although absences, dislike of school, and working part-time all negatively affected the grades of those graduating with competitive or semicompetitive credentials, only absences affected the grades of noncompetitive students. Even then, the magnitude of the effect on grades of not coming to school was considerably less for these students than for the rest.

A pattern thus emerges. A large number of high school students take rather high levels of college prep courses, but their participation is passive, at best. They might as well take high school correspondence courses. These students are playing the *one way to win* game without much enthusiasm. In fact, when asked, they agreed: 75% of those in the Class of 1998 Follow-Up Study who graduated unprepared for college said they wished "they had worked harder while in high school."

Career Uncertainty

Passivity and lack of engagement by academically average students may be partially explained by the fact that, compared with their more academically successful peers, they are less certain about why they took college prep courses in the first place. Indicative of this situation is the degree to which the academically unprepared were significantly more likely to express feelings of career uncertainty. For example, these students were twice as likely to volunteer on the follow-up survey that they wished they had "thought more about their future" while in high school. Likewise, a majority (60%) of all respondents wished that the high school had provided opportunities to explore careers. In fact, a much higher percentage (80%) of those graduating with academically noncompetitive credentials thought this way; this finding suggests a higher level of both career uncertainty and anxiety.

Thus, although we cannot say with certainty that career immaturity or uncertainty was a factor in their lack of academic success, it may be something more than a coincidence that the more successful the students were in the college prep program, the less likely they were to express a need for opportunities to explore careers. Studies of community college undergraduate and graduate students, for example, indicate that at least half of America's postsecondary population indicates their need for assistance with career planning, career choice, or both (Herr & Cramer, 1996). One wonders, then, about these students' level of commitment to preparing for college, in the light of their relative uncertainty about their future. This speculation adds weight to the argument that many pursue college prep because they have been provided with only *one way to win*. It would seem that if they needed guidance, they did not get it in high school. In fact, in high school they were largely asked to take a back seat.

Second-Class Status

If the academically average seem largely uninvolved, it is because they are treated this way within the social framework of the U.S. high school. Basically, they are largely ignored and treated as second-class citizens.

In the true Taylorist tradition, high school educators appear to be preparing the academically less-blessed for future roles as quiescent, anonymous subordinates. As is pointed out in *The Shopping Mall High School* (Powell, Farrar, & Cohen, 1985), these students are relegated to the role of "spectator." They are asked or ordered to sit passively during awards assemblies while their more blessed peers receive all the awards. They are expected to show "school spirit" by filling the stands at pep rallies for more honored student athletes. Even the uniqueness that should fall on those in the academic middle because of enrollment in revered college prep courses does not occur: Today, virtually everyone is enrolled in this curriculum. The awards are reserved now only for those enrolled in honors or advanced placement college prep courses. This Taylorist modus operandi is not lost on students, particularly those relegated to second-class status. As part of the Class of 1998 Follow-Up Study, graduates were asked whether they thought "some students were treated better than others"; 78% of all graduates and 84% of those graduating with noncompetitive credentials responded affirmatively.

How is it possible for nearly half of the teens in any high school to be lost, even when they are in a college prep program of study? Some researchers suggest a masked bias by teachers in favor of the more academically talented. Evidence suggests that teachers do describe and treat the blessed in significantly more positive terms than the less blessed (Oakes, 1985). Yet, in most cases, the situation is probably due more to benign neglect than to covert plots or sinister prejudices. Perhaps there are simply too many teens and too few teachers. Regardless, few would debate that when it comes to academic performance, the standards for those in the academic middle are lower; there is little demand for excellence, and the teens know it.

Low Academic Expectations

As part of the Class of 1998 Follow-Up Study, graduates were asked whether they "wished they had worked harder in high school." Seventy-five percent of academically unprepared students said they wished they had. Equally important, they apparently were not asked to. When asked whether they "felt pressure to get good grades," fewer than half of this group said yes. Even in college prep courses, these students are not held to the same standards as the academically gifted cohort sequestered in honors and AP courses. Homework is a good example.

Although the academically less blessed may not be able to achieve at the same level as the blessed, they should be expected to invest equal amounts of time in trying. One indicator of institutional expectation of effort is whether or not homework is regularly required. Any number of studies have documented the lower amount of homework, if any, expected of less academically blessed students (see Bottoms, Pressons, & Johnson, 1992). Some researchers have gone so far as to suggest that an unwritten deal has been struck between those who make up the academic middle and their teachers. The authors of *The Shopping Mall High School* (Powell et al., 1985) call these agreements "classroom treaties," whereby unmotivated students agree not to hassle the teachers and, in turn, the teachers agree not to hassle them. Thus, much less is required of these students than would be required of more academically able students.

Sedlak (1986) argues that the lack of rigorous academic standards for those in the academic middle, together with the classroom standoff between teachers and those from the academic middle who now enroll in college prep courses, represents a logical adjustment to contradictory social expectations. Specifically, in the face of unrealistic expectations of universal attendance and now universal success in preparing all students for college, high schools simply have adjusted. The academically gifted, those who are blessed with the cognitive skills to succeed in the *one way to win* game, are placed in honors courses and provided with a demanding and rigorous program. The rest, if they choose, are allowed to enroll in college prep courses, but the daily routine and standards within these courses are quite different from those populated by the academically blessed. Honors courses are challenging and competitive, whereas courses for the less blessed are passive, generally unchallenging, and noncompetitive. Debate and cooperative or group learning are common in advanced college prep classes, whereas lectures and predictable routine dominate classes for the average student in the college prep program. When discussion does occur in the regular college prep classes, it is often at the concrete recitation level, whereas in advanced courses, students are challenged to interpret and extrapolate. At both levels, some homework is required, but the complexity and level of thinking required in honors courses is more advanced (Powell et al., 1985). In advanced college prep classes, both the academic content and teacher expectations are what would be expected of those preparing for serious college work. The same cannot be said of regular courses populated by academically average students. This finding explains why many of those who graduate having taken college prep courses still are not prepared to do college work.

Other Ways to Win

In this chapter, the academic credentials of high school graduates have been examined to determine the degree of readiness to pursue the most popular goal after graduation, namely, a 4-year college degree.

Of particular interest was whether high school students were graduating with the advanced academic credentials needed to predict academic success in college. A study of 1998 high school graduates from seven public high schools, where virtually all were supposedly preparing for college, revealed that, at most, only 27% earned the academically advanced credentials normally associated with admissions and success at Level 1 colleges (those that are still selective and rigorous). At best, another 24% graduated with credentials that might predict readiness to do higher education academic work at Level 2 institutions, those that accept virtually everyone. The remaining students graduated with credentials that suggested inadequate preparation for higher education.

Of particular importance to those seeking to create *other ways to win* is evidence that simply enrolling these students in traditional college prep high school courses is not instructionally effective. Although students may take the courses, they do not necessarily master the content. Furthermore, this group is largely unengaged in the high school curriculum in general, perhaps because they are largely ignored or unchallenged by high school teachers. These students report not being pressed to do well in high school and wishing they had worked harder. They also wished they had thought more about their future and had been given more opportunities to explore careers while in high school. This information suggests that, compared with their more academically successful peers, they lack career maturity. The point is that if educators are to create legitimate *other ways to win*, it will be necessary to devise not just postsecondary alternatives but also focused, rigorous academics that prepare students to succeed by providing well-planned and focused career exploration. Evidence suggests that this creation calls for higher expectations and new instructional approaches, all of which are explored in detail in Part 3.

Data reviewed in this chapter demonstrate the unavoidable conclusion that, even in elite public high schools, only about half of graduating students are even minimally prepared to do college-level work. One can assume that, in lesser high schools, the percentage is lower. Yet, like their counterparts across the United States, faced with only *one way to win*, most students went on to higher education anyway, mostly to 4-year colleges or to 2-year general studies transfer programs. Clearly, this decision by those with noncompetitive academic credentials seems unrealistic and thus very risky. These students seem to require better alternatives or *other ways to win*. Of course, the validity of this argument necessitates evidence, such as data about the level of success experienced by academically average students in higher education. This topic is the focus of Chapter 5.

Note

1. Mark Pitsch, 1994, p. 7. Copyright © 1994, *Education Week*; reprinted by permission.

5

Winners and Losers in
the *One Way to Win* Game

*Diplomas from most American universities are a devalued currency in the
market place. It no longer means what it used to.*
Michael Garber, Hudson Institute

I f enrollment projections are any indication, 4-year college enrollments will continue to climb through 2007. This may well be one of those rare cases, however, where more may not be better. By the late 1990s, some writers were suggesting that so many were pursuing a 4-year college degree that its value, particularly in the social sciences and liberal arts, was about equal to a high school diploma.

It is argued in this book that continued growth of baccalaureate education requires public scrutiny. If increased enrollments are resulting in more students' entering 4-year colleges unprepared, ending up in remedial courses, and flunking out after accumulating significant student loan debt, or if greater percentages of those who do graduate end up underemployed, then this growth is, in fact, harmful. The purpose of this chapter is to provide evidence to objectively answer the question, Among those who pursue the *one way to win* paradigm, how many win and how many lose? If the justification is to provide opportunity, just how much opportunity is being provided?

SECTION I

Remedial Education and
College Dropouts:
The First Losers

The conventional wisdom of *one way to win* is the belief that the only route—at least the only socially acceptable route—to the American dream involves getting at least a baccalaureate degree in the hope that it will lead to a job in the professional ranks. The majority of today's high school students are taking college prep courses. Aided by open admissions at most institutions of higher education, most enroll in 4-year colleges or 2-year programs that hold a promise of leading to a 4-year degree. This is true despite the fact that many young people graduate from high school with academic credentials demonstrating a lack of preparation for college-level work. Is the unprecedented growth in higher education enrollments, particularly in programs leading to a 4-year degree, a positive development? And is this a wise investment of both individual and public funds? The answers seem to depend, first, on the degree to which a reasonable number of those who enroll are academically prepared and how many graduate.

Academic Ability to Benefit

One test of the wisdom of *one way to win* for all and, conversely, of the need to create other economically legitimate and socially acceptable alternatives to pursuing a 4-year degree, is how well freshmen, particularly those from the academic middle, perform in college. Our review of the effectiveness of college prep programs in Chapter 4 gives us reason to expect that many who head off to college are not ready to do college-level work. College faculty, when polled, agree: Only 20% of faculty at baccalaureate institutions agreed that incoming freshmen were adequately prepared in "written and oral communication skills." Only 15% felt the same way about undergraduate preparation in mathematics ("International Survey," 1994). Perhaps the best evidence of the academic deficiency of many entering freshmen at all types of higher education institutions is the number who must take remedial courses during their freshman year.

Figure 5.1 Remedial Education in Higher Education, Fall 1995

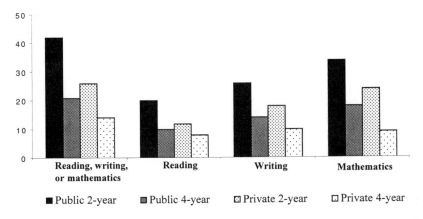

SOURCE: National Center for Education Statistics, 1998.

Remedial Education
in Higher Education

One of the best kept secrets in higher education is the large amount of course work taken by entering freshman that does not count toward a degree. Parents in particular are often shocked when they find out that their teenager, who got mostly B grades in high school, is taking remedial courses in college. According to the American Council on Education (1999), 90% of private colleges and virtually all public institutions now offer remedial courses. The exact number of students taking these courses is not easy to find. One NCES study (National Center for Education Statistics, 1988) found that 41% of students at 2-year institutions and 22% at 4-year institutions were taking one or more remedial courses (see Figure 5.1); however, the data were provided by the institutions, thus the possibility of underreporting.

Our purpose is not to question the merits of offering remedial education at the collegiate level (see Clark, 1962). But we do ask, Just how effective is this remediation? Although colleges report that three fourths of participating students pass these courses, it does not seem to matter. Having to take remedial education courses is a strong predictor of one thing: dropping out. An Ohio study found that only

TABLE 5.1 Higher Education Freshmen: Remedial Courses and Sophomore Status, Class of 1998 Follow-Up Study

%	Remedial English	Remedial Math	Any Remedial	Achieved Sophomore Status
Unprepared	22%	32%		
Marginally prepared	18%	6%	25%	68%

SOURCE: Gray & Xiaoli, 1999.

about a third of students who were required to take remedial courses ever graduated.

Of particular interest to this discussion is what happens to those from the academic middle. How many must take remedial courses? One answer is provided by the Class of 1998 Follow-Up Study (see Table 5.1).

Respondents in the study were asked several questions to determine their academic success in the freshman year. As a group, the participation rate in remedial education was a little less than the NCES reported average of 29%. Few students from the prepared and about a fifth of those from the marginally prepared took remedial education. However, when one looks at the students we are interested in—those from the academic middle—the numbers are much higher. About half of the unprepared group were taking remedial courses. Similar to other national data, mathematics was the most common area of weakness.

So, what is the point? Our intent is not to point the finger at high schools for poor preparation. In all fairness, it must be said that high schools prepare well those blessed with the academic ability to do legitimate college-level work. Although we could fault the colleges for admitting ill-prepared students, college administrators would argue that they are providing equal opportunity through open admissions. Instead, then, our intention is to suggest that if these large numbers of students are not prepared to do baccalaureate degree academic work, then maybe—just maybe—they should be doing something else. And if, given some legitimate, socially valued alternatives that make economic sense, perhaps many of these students *would* do something else. Without other choices, what happens to those who start college having to take remedial courses? Many fail. As Burton Clark (1962) argued, "The initial move in a cooling out process is pre-entrance testing: low scores lead poorly qualified students into remedial classes . . . which slows the students moving into bona fide courses . . . and cast doubt (regarding ever graduating)" (pp. 569-577).

Although in Clark's time, remedial courses were confined to 2-year junior colleges, today they exist virtually everywhere in higher education. Their effect, however, has not changed over time. Enrollment in remedial courses is the first sign of trouble in the *one way to win* game. The second sign is the number returning home after completion of the freshman year who have not earned a sufficient number of credits to be classified as sophomores.

College Dropouts

Of high school graduates who go directly on to higher education, the first losers are those who must take remedial education courses. The second group of losers is those who fail to persist to graduate. These include many who take remedial education, and also many who do not. How many actually graduate?

Table 5.2 shows the percentage of students who actually graduate with some type of a degree 5 years after they start, based on the degree they were pursuing. Of those who pursue a 4-year college degree, about half (46%) graduate with a bachelor's degree within 5 years. Some do not earn a 4-year degree but get instead a 1- or 2-year degree; thus, of those who start a 4-year degree program, 54% end up with some type of degree or certificate after 5 years. A higher percentage of those who start at 4-year institutions (57%) earn a degree than those who start in transfer programs at 2-year institutions (7.9%). In fact, of those who start a transfer program at a 2-year college, only 29% earn any type of degree 5 years later.

Of importance to this discussion is what happens to those from the academic middle who start a 4-year degree program. Lacking

TABLE 5.2 Highest Degree Obtained Within 5 Years

I. By Students Seeking a Bachelor's Degree

Level of First Institution	*Highest Degree Completed in 5 Years (%)*			
	Bachelor's	*Associate*	*Certificate*	*Any*
Total all institutions	45.8	5.1	3.3	54.3
4-year colleges	57.1	2.5	2.1	61.7
2-year colleges	7.9	13.9	7.2	29.0

II. By Students Seeking a 2-Year Degree or Certificate

Degree	*Highest Degree Completed in 5 Years (%)*			
	Bachelor's	*Associate*	*Certificate*	*Any*
Associate degree	7.5	23.7	11.4	42.6
Certificate	0.5	4.3	49.7	54.5

SOURCE: NCES, 1990 Beginning Postsecondary Students Longitudinal Study, Second Follow-Up (BPS:90/94).

competitive academic skills, a high percentage (in the class of 1988 it was over half) of those from the academic middle start a 4-year program at a 2-year institution. Yet, as indicated in Table 5.2, those who choose this route mostly fail. Data from the Follow-up Study of the Class of 1998 complement these findings. Among the unqualified group who were in higher education, only half had achieved sophomore status after one year.

At the same time, Table 5.2 provides insight into *other ways to win*. Of those who pursue an associate degree or certificate at a 2-year institution, the success rate is about the same as those for the more academically blessed who enroll in 4-year colleges. This suggests that the persistence rate is dramatically better for those from the academic middle if they pursue a certificate or associate degree program, most of which are typically career related.

Of course, students drop out of college for a variety of reasons. Some of these would exist even if there were *other ways to win*. Of interest here are the variables that cause students to drop out and that can be influenced in high school. One way to focus on these variables is to examine students who drop out during their freshman year, because, arguably, these are the ones whose failure is most related to their high school preparation.

Many parents of college freshmen spend that first year in various stages of apprehension, waiting for the dreaded call from college. They sense, without being told, another one of higher education's well-guarded secrets: Basically, one third of all college freshmen drop out during their freshman year (Levitz & Noel, 1985). Many drop out before they even really begin. If the number of all freshman dropouts is subtracted from the number who leave between semesters, half of the rest drop out during the first 6 weeks. It is a mistake to think that these students simply flunk out. In fact, some data suggest that the first-year dropout rates for college freshmen are just as high for academically able students as for marginal students.

The huge number of entering freshmen who fail to return the following year suggests that many youth are making what they later decide was a bad decision. They do not necessarily fail; that can take a couple of years. Instead, they drift away. They have played the college game and made everyone happy, but high school graduation is over and the pressures are not as intense; they throw in the towel and leave school, but not without costs. According to the General Accounting Office (GAO) (1991), an important predictor of those who will default on student loan debts is whether they failed to complete their first year. Thus, for at least one third of all college freshmen, going to college proves, in the first year, to be a very expensive mistake. Furthermore, only about one third of all who matriculate graduate in 4 years, and only about one half ever graduate at all. One wonders how many of these, even among those who are academically gifted, did not really want to go in the first place and would have made other choices if they had had *other ways to win*.

Of course, about half of those who start a 4-year degree program actually graduate. If they are white or Asian, about 6 of 10 graduate; if they are persons of color, about 3 of 10 graduate. So now it is time to deliver the final wake-up call to those promoting attendance at a 4-year college. The bad news is that almost half of those who do graduate from college will end up underemployed.

SECTION II

Underemployed College Graduates:
The Second Losers

National survey data (see Table 1.1) of both high school graduates and entering college freshmen show that the principal reason for going to college is to get a better job. In fact, economic uncertainty regarding future employment opportunities and the conclusion that only a 4-year college degree offers any opportunities have been largely responsible for the growth in college enrollments since the early 1980s. Overwhelmingly, high school graduates place their hopes for a secure economic future in one set of occupations, the professions. In a 1992 study of graduating seniors, 49.3% of males and 68.8% of females expected to be employed in the professions (see Table 1.2). No other occupational choice was even close. Only 6.7% were inspired either to own their own businesses or to be managers or technicians (6.0%). Only 2.8% expected to enter the well-paying skilled trades. For all practical purposes, everyone has the same career plan, and its folly is obvious. Major league baseball players make lots of money, but (a) not everyone has the talent to be one and (b) even if everyone did, there are only so many jobs in the big leagues to go around. The same is true for professional work.

The public in general and students and parents in particular seem to have faith that if one earns a 4-year degree that includes a professional credential, such as a teaching certificate or a law degree, a job will be waiting. The assumption is that the demand for professionals will increase to accommodate the rising percentage of the population who hold these credentials. By the late 1990s, signs indi-

TABLE 5.3 Comparison of Occupation Supply and Demand by Higher Education Credential to the Year 2007

	Supply	Demand	% Underemployed
First professional	79,300	58,200	27
Doctorate	47,900	46,000	3
Master's	450,000	43,000	90
Bachelor's	1,268,000	734,300	43

SOURCE: *Monthly Labor Review* (November, 1997).

cated that this faith was not well placed. For example, by the early 1990s, the popular press was carrying cover stories such as that in *U.S News and World Report* (Elfin, 1993), which asked rhetorically, "Does College Still Pay?" The author of this article went on to argue that the "economic argument for college is not as compelling as it once was; the problem: too many graduates, too few jobs, and declining relative wages" (p. 96).

The Labor Market Outlook for College Graduates

Students, parents, and all those promoting the *one way to win* strategy take note. Evidence suggests that, even among those who persist to graduate, many will end up losers. Projections by the U.S. Department of Education regarding degrees awarded annually, with projections by the U.S. Department of Labor regarding the demand for jobs at various levels of education (see Table 5.3), predict a dramatic oversupply of 4-year college graduates.

Table 5.4 provides a comparison of projected supply of degrees awarded at the bachelor's level or above and the labor market demand for individuals educated at these levels. Our main interest is

TABLE 5.4 Projected Average Annual Job Openings, 1990-2005

	Openings	Number of Credentials Awarded	Net Openings
Professional managerial			
Executive, administration	436,000	506,830	-70,830
Construction managers	7,000	825	+6175
Marketing, advertising, and public relations managers	23,000	66,416	-43,416
Professional specialty	623,000	1,120,063	-497,063
Physical scientists	8,000	35,163	-27,163
Lawyers	28,006	44,314	-16,308
Technical			
Technicians	183,000	212,767	-29,767
Health	79,000	71,804	+7,196
Engineering	52,000	85,611	-33,611
Blue-collar technical			
Craft, precision metal, and specialized repair	455,000	133,057	+321,943
Mechanics, installers, repairers	160,000	91,758	+68,242
Service occupations	882,000	237,062	+644,938
Operators, laborers	477,000	41,504	+435,496
Farming, forestry, fishing	90,000	14,547	+75,453

SOURCE: Data compiled from Eck, A. (1993).

the 4-year degree level. The annual demand for 4-year college graduates is substantial: 734,000 jobs annually. It sounds like a lot until one takes note of the supply numbers. Annually, the nation's colleges are projected to graduate 1.268 million individuals. The implication is clear. On average, 43 of every 100 that persist to get a degree will not find commensurate employment. This amounts to over a half a million persons annually and, of course, this number compounds each year. Thus, between 1998 and 2006, there are projected to be well over 4 million underemployed 4-year college graduates.

The stark reality is that, while the percentage of teens trying the *one way to win* paradigm increases each year and the percentage of young adults that have a 4-year degree grows each year, the percentage of all work that requires education at this level does not. Despite all the rhetoric about the need for further education, labor studies suggest that the percentage of all work that requires a 4-year degree is only 13%, which is only 1% higher than it was 10 years ago (Silvestri, 1997). In fact, only 23% of all jobs in the United States require education beyond a 2-year degree; 40% of all work can be learned in only 2 weeks.

Thus, in a NCES study of recent 4-year college graduates, *Baccalaureate and Beyond* (McCormick & Knepper, 1996), almost half said that they held jobs that did not require a 4-year degree. Certainly some will find commensurate employment in the future, but each year another half million join the ranks of the underemployed. Therefore, if the projections are at all accurate, more and more will graduate but never find work commensurate with their 4-year degree.

The mismatch between projected demand and supply of credentialed college graduates becomes even more dramatic when one looks at data for selected occupations. Table 5.4 provides the projected average annual job openings for occupational groups, the number of education and training credentials awarded annually, and the resultant net demand or surplus of candidates. Notice immediately the projected net demand in professional occupations. Most high school graduates who go to college say they expect to work in the professional ranks, but there clearly are not enough jobs to go around. For example, the economy is expected to generate 623,000 jobs in the professional specialty category, but it is also projected that the higher education system will award more than 1.1 million professional undergraduate and graduate degrees. Considering that these supply figures do not include other sources of employees for these professional jobs, such as professionals trained abroad, it is clear that, at best, only one of two who prepare for the specialized professional ranks will find commensurate employment.

The sobering bottom line for 49.3% of male and 68.8% of female high school graduates with ambitions to enter the professions (Table 1.2) is that, at best, even among those who actually graduate from college, there will be twice as many individuals graduating with professional credentials than there will be jobs available. In fact, the data reveal many widespread misconceptions about the need for certain types of professionals. Although the oversupply of lawyers is widely known, the popular belief is that there is a national shortage of scientists, engineers, and related workers. This is a misconception (see Table 5.4). Even in the hard sciences, the supply of graduates greatly exceeds the demand, a fact that leads some, such as Rustum Roy (1992), world-renowned solid state scientist, to argue that the shortage of people in the sciences is just a myth created by the National Science Foundation to obtain greater funding from Congress. Similarly, when Congress asked the GAO to investigate claims of a dramatic shortage of college trained information technology workers in the late 1990s, the GAO reported that the demand had been grossly exaggerated. As will be discussed in Chapter 7, though serious shortages did exist, they were primarily for technicians trained at the prebaccalaureate level. In fact, the only major professional occupations in which demand will greatly exceed supply are physicians and dentists (Eck, 1993).

The bad news is not confined to the professions. When looking at other occupational groups normally associated with 4-year college-level preparation, similar oversupplies may be found. An example is professional managerial occupations. In this category, demand will exceed supply (see Table 5.4). A close look at the managerial occupational group, however, reveals some interesting exceptions that hint at *other ways to win*. For example, there is an oversupply of people preparing to be marketing, advertising, and public relations managers—popular majors at 4-year colleges. Conversely, the demand for individuals with the skills necessary to manage construction projects, which are well-paid positions, greatly exceeds the supply.

These positions do not require a 4-year college degree. They may not be as glamorous, but they are both high-paying and offer good opportunities for advancement, a fact discussed in Chapter 7.

SECTION III

More Losers?
Those Who Prepare for
College but Go to Work Instead

The percentage of high school graduates that pursue full-time employment directly after high school has declined dramatically. Yet on average, 2 of every 10 go to work full time and, in some locales and in some states, it is more that half. Significantly, more than half of those who pursue full-time employment did not take vocational education in high school, but in fact were quasi-college prep students. How do these students who took college prep courses fare in the labor market? The question becomes important in determining the need for *other ways to win*. To probe this issue, we return to the Class of 1998 Follow-Up Study.

Dead-End Jobs
for Those Without
Vocational Education

Researchers conducting the Class of 1998 Follow-Up Study (Gray & Xiaoli, 1999) were particularly interested in the postsecondary experiences of graduates who did not take vocational education but went to work full time. Indicative of the persuasiveness of the *one way to win* press, 60% of this group had taken the SAT. This group contained a small percentage of very academically able students. The majority (82%), however, graduated unqualified for college. Those who went to work but had not been enrolled in vocational education course work were the most marginal of college prep students. How did they do? Not well. Their average yearly income was $16,303, which would be poverty level for a family of four. Of course, many were earning even less: One third were making between $8,000 and $15,000. The majority were working in services and transportation industries, followed by food service or retailing and manufacturing.

Importantly, the experiences of this group, particularly those who graduated with academically noncompetitive credentials, were significantly poorer than the experiences of those who took vocational education. Those completing vocational education programs of study were less apt to be unemployed and earned higher salaries. No doubt, the latter resulted from the fact that vocational education graduates were more likely to be employed in work that required some prior skills. Vocational education graduates, for example, were more likely to have found employment in the skilled trades, health occupations, and food industries (not to be confused with fast-food service jobs).

Almost all of the Class of 1998 in the labor force worked in small firms: 39% in firms with fewer than 19 employees, 79% in firms with fewer than 500 employees. This finding is important because of the often-heard argument that high school students do not need courses that teach job skills because employers will provide on-the-job training. Small firms cannot afford to provide on-the-job training and are the least likely to do so (Carnevale, Gainer, & Villet, 1990). Indeed, studies indicate that American employers, compared with their foreign counterparts, invest less in new entrants to the workforce and in only limited cases provide extensive on-the-job training. (Hilton, 1991). Many employers, particularly but not exclusively small firms, tend to expect young workers to come prepared with the necessary employment skills (Herr, 1995). Thus, it was not surprising to find that only 22% of those in the labor force reported receiving formal training. The importance of training and its relationship to work that pays a living wage were illustrated by the data: Those who reported having been trained by their employer were earning on average $19,982 a year, versus $10,000 for those who had not. Confirming other studies (Gray & Wang, 1989), the data suggest that those who think high school graduates will be trained by employers are largely mistaken and that those who need training the most are least likely to get it unless it is in high school.

In summary, what can be said about those who take the traditional college prep program of study but go to work? Do they win or lose as a result of preparing for the *one way to win* game instead of for full-time employment? Compared with those who take vocational education, they primarily lose. In general, they end up in unskilled jobs in small firms, mostly in the service industries. They receive no formal training and earn only minimum wage. As a group, they are more likely to be unemployed, and, if they are employed, they are more likely to earn less than students who took a comprehensive vocational education program. For those seeking to create *other ways to win*, it is important, therefore, to note that the most at risk among those who went to work are those from the academic middle who graduated without any work experiences.

Other Ways to Win

In this chapter, data from the postsecondary experiences of recent high school graduates have been studied to evaluate the merits of the *one way to win* philosophy. The data suggest the wisdom of questioning the *one way to win* paradigm among both those who head off to 4-year colleges and those who, without adequate preparation, go to work. The losers outnumber the winners.

For example, the data reveal that, of those who begin a BA program, only slightly more than half of whites and Asians and fewer than half of other people of color graduate. Furthermore, of the group that does graduate, 43% will still lose because the economy will provide too little college-level work. When one looks just at those who aspire to the professions, the majority of whom are women, the odds of winning are even worse. Of those preparing for the professions—accountants, chemists, elementary school teachers, engineers, and so forth—only one of two will find work.

Who will be the winners? Common sense and good research suggest the winners can be identified in high school. The winners will be those who graduate with academically competitive credentials that enable them to go to better colleges; these credentials will, in turn, give them advantages in the labor market when competing for a limited number of professional and other 4-year college-level jobs.

Who will be the losers? The losers likely will be among those who graduated from the academic middle—those who were pressed into attending 4-year colleges even though they lacked adequate academic preparation or the ability to succeed. The losers will also include those who, for whatever reason, prepared in high school to go to college but went to work instead. Thus, it is difficult not to conclude that losers outnumber winners in the *one way to win* game.

We make one final point. If so many young people in the academic middle are being hurt at great cost to themselves, to their parents, and even to the United States as a whole by the *one way to win* paradigm, and if those who need help the most are hurt the most, then why isn't corrective action being taken? The answer lies in the politics of the academically average in U.S. high schools, which is the topic of Chapter 6.

6

Who Cares?
The Politics of Average Students

*A great many people think they are thinking when they are merely
rearranging their prejudices.*

William James (1842-1910)

In terms of achieving their expressed postsecondary education and career goals, more than 50% of all high school graduates fail. Nationwide, 85% of high school graduates want to obtain a 4-year college degree, but only 40% graduate with the academically advanced credentials to indicate adequate preparation for legitimate college-level academic work. Most (72%) high school graduates go on to college, most to 4-year colleges, despite inadequate academic preparation. Thus, it is not surprising to find that 30% or more have to take remedial courses sometime during their freshman year in college. Six years later, only about 50% actually graduate with a 4-year degree. The rest of the students "cool out" of the higher education system, but not before most have accumulated significant debt.

Meanwhile, the employment prospects for those who do persist and obtain a 4-year degree worsen. Whereas in the past, one in every five persons with college degrees failed to find commensurate employment, today it is almost one in two. Although 4-year college graduates do not go unemployed, more and more end up in jobs that require only a high school diploma or less. Meanwhile, the nation faces an unprecedented shortage of technicians trained at the prebaccalaureate level. The nation's firms search the world to fill high skill/ high wage technical occupations, while growing numbers of American college graduates end up in low-paying occupations struggling to pay off student loan debts.

Not a very pretty picture, is it? Yet few want to talk about it. It is the "quiet dilemma." Quiet because students, parents, and the education community are largely silent. Meanwhile, politicians continue to speak and act as though it were the 1980s; they sense little advantage in taking on a problem no one wants to acknowledge even exists. Others take financial advantage of the situation. It is the strange politics of *one way to win* or the "must go to college" mentality. More specifically, it is the strange politics of "average students," the most common victims of providing only *one way to win*.

SECTION I

High School Politics and the Academically Average

It is important to understand that average students—those who make up the academic middle, those hurt most by *one way to win*— have no advocates either locally or nationally. The Washington, DC, advocacy (a fancy name for lobbying) scene is a good illustration. At least 30 groups promote themselves as advocates for children with special needs. There are lobbyists for college students, for Ivy League colleges, for land-grant universities, and for unemployed engineers, to name a few. But as far as we know, there is no advocacy group for academically average students.

Whereas the academically blessed have many advocates—for example, their parents who serve on public school boards, high school teachers who love to teach advanced placement and honors courses, and school administrators who see admissions at prestigious colleges as the zenith of educational effectiveness—average teens have no one. Whereas special needs students have an army of advocates and laws to safeguard their rights, average students have neither—a situation that led the authors of *The Shopping Mall High School* (Powell et al., 1985) to label them the "unspecial."

In reporting the results of an ethnographic case study of several high schools, Powell et al. (1985) were struck by the invisibility of average students; in fact, they were so invisible that high school educators had difficulty describing them:

> Indeed, one important characteristic is the very absence of precision (in high school teachers' minds) about exactly who they (the unspecial) are. They were variously the "invisible people," "the middle of the class," and "that great gray-mass area," those who don't belong anywhere, the people who don't fit into any . . . categories. (p. 174)

Powell et al. go on to confirm the argument made here: The unspecial are the majority:

> Words like *average, middle, normal,* and *regular* were often used to describe quite different kinds of adolescents. Some enrolled in college-preparatory programs but were not in advanced or honors courses and therefore were no longer special because post-secondary education was a mass expectation. Others saw the unspecial as a contemporary version of traditional "general" students—shaped neither by clear college expectations or a focused vocational education program. To others the unspecial were those on the top end of the bottom spectrum. (p. 175)

And they have no advocates:

> Another fundamental characteristic of the unspecial is that they have no important allies or advocates. Top track students are blessed with a strong constituency of parents. The handicapped and those with a highly focused vocational interest, even the unruly, had their spokespeople, usually organized lobbies or political groups that generated money or mandates from legislatures and courts. (p. 176)

Data from the Economic Policy Institute (Rothstein, 1997) confirm this observation. Between 1967 and 1996, the percentage of school budgets spent on regular education (that part of the budget that supports education for the academic middle) dropped from 80% to 57%. Meanwhile, the percentage of the budget spent on special education, bilingual education, and other programs for special students increased from 4% to 22%. In other words, while education budgets have grown over the years, the percentage of dollars spent on those in the academic middle has actually decreased.

The parents of these youth are largely silent, either because of the feeling that no news from school is good news or because they lack the savvy or the combativeness to effect change. For example, whereas parents' organizations are the norm at all elementary schools and are typical at middle or junior highs, they seldom exist at the high school level. Why? One reason is that high school educators do not encourage them. Another reason is that the parents of the silent majority are, by now, almost completely silent. It's not that they don't care; they just seem to give up. As one counselor said, "Most parents are too busy trying to survive (raising a teenager) to try to tell the schools what to do" (Powell et al., 1985, p. 177). This is too bad because high school educators also have largely given up trying to advise students, particularly those from the academic middle, what to do.

Why High School Educators
Look the Other Way

Conversations with high school principals, counselors, and teachers (the authors of this book have, at various times, served in all of these positions) leave little doubt that these professionals are aware of the growing number of academically average youth in the college prep programs who do not do very well but then still go on to 4-year colleges. In fact, guidance counselors are increasingly amazed at the ease with which students with mediocre academic credentials gain admittance into what used to be fairly selective colleges and universities. They also are well aware that few high school students know why they are going to college except that their parents want it, everyone else expects it, and there appear to be no alternatives. Here we get to the heart of the matter.

High schools are public institutions and, as such, are quite responsive—better yet, vulnerable—to community desires. The old saw among superintendents of schools was and still is that as long as the band plays on tune, the football team has a winning season, and the students get into college, the public is happy. It's true. National data indicate that most parents want their children to go to college, and in this day and age there is little stopping them. In the light of the politics that exists today in most high schools, few principals are willing to deliver this message: Many students enrolled in the college prep program are not prepared to do baccalaureate-level work. In a society in which "kill the messenger" is the rule, the lack of willingness to deliver this message is understandable. In fact, parents often do not wake up until the dreaded SAT or ACT college admissions test scores arrive. Meanwhile, school personnel are thankful that this insight is coming from someone else.

Are Guidance Counselors the Villains?

At this point in discussions of the unrealistic postsecondary plans of high school youth, many point their fingers at guidance counselors, who are viewed as the professionals responsible for reality therapy. Realistically, parents have only themselves to blame. As one counselor explained,

> For years, all we have heard is cases of successful college graduates who report that their guidance counselor told them not to go to college. After 20 years of this abuse and criticism, most counselors are a bit gun-shy about presenting any information, let alone advising that anyone should not go on to college.

Because the kill-the-messenger attitude pervades the situation, counselors, like other school personnel, end up looking the other way. It is easy to understand such attitudes. An increasingly frequent story told by counselors is about the calls they get from irate parents because the counselor even suggested to their child that they consider anything other than the *one way to win* strategy. No parent, principal, or school board wants to hear this type of information. The open admissions policies at many colleges and universities enable all who want a degree from a 4-year college to get in anyway.

One other issue is more difficult for high school educators to duck: How can students be in a college prep program of study and get passing grades, yet end up in remedial courses in college?

Grade Inflation

Periodically, the media write about something called *grade inflation*. The term means that grades go up without requisite evidence that learning is increasing too; in fact, data often suggest just the opposite. For example, although SAT entrance test scores have stagnated over the years, the grade point averages reported by entering college freshmen keep going up. In 1969, 12% of entering college freshmen said they had A averages, compared with 32% in 1998. Meanwhile, during the same period, the percentage reporting a C average in high school went from 32% to 8%. Similarly, 92% of all freshmen entered college with a B average or better, yet a survey of college professors revealed that fewer than 10% thought that students were adequately prepared in math. Such data (Samuelson, 1991) do not make sense: Grade point averages increase, yet objective assessments of readiness to do college-level work do not show similar increases. What is going on? Some authors (Sedlak, 1986) suggest that a stalemate exists between teachers and the academically average youth in their classes. Teachers ask little of academically average students; in return, these students ask little of their teachers.

The Stalemate in
High School Classrooms

Understanding the stalemate that exists between high school teachers and average students in college prep classes requires an appreciation of the impossible catch-22 situation that high school faculty find themselves in because of public demands. High schools are asked to do the impossible: Be rigorous but ensure that everyone gets grades that will enable him or her to get into college. Maybe it is possible for high schools to do both—high school bashers have made careers of suggesting that such action is possible—but under the circumstances, it is not. But as the experience at colleges (where most high school bashers work) has shown, standards are difficult to maintain when a priority is keeping the universities and colleges full. This point was aptly illustrated by cartoonist Garry Trudeau in his panel about a fraternity member who sued the university because he got a B+ instead of the expected A. Obviously, problems with grade inflation are not confined to high schools.

The public simply will not accept one basic reality: If a normal population of high school students is put into college prep courses that carry high academic performance standards (not to be confused with high expectations, which should be the norm for all students), not everyone is going to do well. Thus, if everyone is to do well, the only solution, at least given the current student-to-teacher ratio in U.S. high schools, is to lower standards. This is exactly what is occurring in the college prep classes taken by those in the academic middle of U.S. high schools. Academically average students and their parents ask no questions as long as everyone gets above average grades and into college; today, that is virtually ensured. If no one looks too closely at the learning that may or may not be taking place in classes populated by the academic middle, then everyone is content. One reason for this contentment is that the academically blessed receive a different college prep curriculum—one with real standards and failing grades—offered under code names such as advanced placement or honors courses.

The politics of the situation allows no other solution. The public wants all students in the high schools to graduate with high academic credentials so that they can go to college, but for a variety of reasons this task cannot be done. All but a few of these reasons are outside the schools' control, so high school faculty compromise; they offer a real "AP" or "honors" college prep program for those who have the ability to do it, and a less rigorous college prep curriculum for those who cannot or will not do as well. In the latter classes, teachers ask less of the students; in return, students and parents do not hassle the teachers. This standoff will not be easy to change as long as *one way to win* goes unchallenged.

SECTION II

Taking the High Ground:
The Role of Elected Officials

Whereas the *one way to win* paradigm is costing the government billions, hindering economic growth, and resulting in more youth failing than succeeding, one might expect elected officials to speak out about the need to consider alternatives to a 4-year college education. As columnist Robert Samuelson suggested, no doubt with tongue in cheek, all they had to do to solve the problem was announce they will no longer support higher education budgets without performance standards. And that they will no longer fool our students or waste taxpayer's money by sending people to college who are not ready (Samuleson, 1991, p. 44). Not surprisingly, none have taken his advice. Some states are now looking at higher education expenditures in relation to strategic economic development plans. But, by and large, more money for college has become a safe bread-and-butter issue for elected officials; in 1999, state support for higher education, most of which goes to baccalaureate education, increased by record amounts.

When it comes to *one way to win*, the rhetoric is classic political "smoke and mirrors," at least at the federal level. Congress passes legislation that increases student aid, and then its members hit the campaign trail to bring the good news to their constituents. They fail to tell the whole story, however: Although Congress has passed a bill to increase student aid benefits, there is no money to fund it.

In the light of the political "hay" to be made from supporting the *one way to win* mentality, it is clearly unrealistic to think the federal government will urge the public to consider alternatives to a 4-year degree leading to a career in the professional ranks. In fact, often the political returns from promoting college attendance are so high that they actually lead to proposals that make no sense. For example, the Clinton administration proposed a payback schedule for direct student loans that did not cover loan interest; over time, then, student loans would actually increase in size!

One final and important point should be made regarding politicians' use of the *one way to win* mentality to increase public approval of their performance. By doing so, they in effect lend considerable credence to the validity of the *one way to win* paradigm. When the president of the United States asserts that anyone who wants to go to college should be able to, the message is interpreted in a far larger context than may have been intended. In the country's classrooms and households, the message means that everyone *should* go to college. Some believe it even insinuates that something is wrong with anyone who does not aspire to college.

SECTION III

Behind the Scenes:
Those With Vested Interests

Each year, higher education in the United States is a billion-dollar business. Revenues for higher education institutions alone are now over $120 billion. This amount may be just the tip of the iceberg because untold billions are generated by products and services related to higher education. College sports on national television, college and financial planners, money lenders, T-shirt manufacturers, textbook publishers, beer distributors, and providers of cram courses for entrance tests, to cite a few, all add up to staggering amounts. Thus, colleges and universities have become big business, and, like all businesses, a steady supply of customers is essential. The point is that, although most endorse *one way to win* because they believe it is sound advice for today's youth, others promote the value of college because their jobs depend on it.

No doubt, the largest vested interest in *one way to win* is the higher education community itself. Higher education is a huge service industry. It sells a service (education)—or more accurately, products (degrees)—employs people, and portrays itself as meeting a need and creating opportunity. If someone dropped in from another world and observed this activity, however, these efforts would more resemble marketers' efforts to create a need for a product in a saturated market.

Obviously, all is not well in this multibillion-dollar enterprise. The industry has overexpanded, classes are underenrolled, dorm rooms are empty, and revenue is down. Thus, recruitment and retention, not excellence, are the priorities at all but a few colleges. Although administrators at most colleges act as if admissions were selective, admissions are truly selective at only about 250 of the more than 3,000 institutions of higher education. In fact, most higher education institutions practice open admissions. Most take the best that apply even if the best of these are not well qualified to do college work; as the adage goes, "Poor students are better than no students." What other explanation is there for the fact that 95% of all public 4-year colleges "offer" (a code word for *require*) remedial courses for entering students (College Entrance Board, 1993)?

One major tactic used by higher education in its increasingly sophisticated marketing efforts to keep colleges and universities full is to reinforce and play off the *one way to win* mentality. These efforts have been very successful. Opportunity and college have become synonymous, thanks in part to these efforts. Suffice it to say that higher education is a strong political force working overtly and covertly to sell and perpetuate *one way to win*. Questions about the sincerity of these efforts are left to the reader to decide. The point is that those who seek to promote *other ways to win* should understand that the United States has an oversupply of baccalaureate degree-granting colleges. (Between 1980 and 1990, the number of public and private baccalaureate-level colleges actually increased despite a decreasing number of high school graduates.) You can expect these institutions to push hard the concept, *one way to win*.

One final group deserves mention among those with a vested interest in *one way to win:* the money lenders and financial planners for whom college mania has become a source of growth and profit. Need money for college? Plan now for college, ask about student loans. Are tuition bills due? Consider a home equity loan. These messages are heard day after day. A house used to be the largest purchase made by a family; now, for many, it is their children's education. By promoting their services, these financial institutions are reinforcing the message and keeping public faith in higher education alive and well; after all, doing so is a dollar-and-cents issue.

Other Ways to Win

In this chapter, we have explored the political realities behind the apparent lack of public concern for the plight of those from the academic middle of high school graduating classes. Aware of no other socially acceptable and economically promising alternatives, many in this group are heading off to college despite being unprepared for it. Most never finish, however, but are successful in accumulating significant student loan debt. Yet, no one seems to voice much concern. There are few, if any, advocates for these students; teachers largely ignore them, and their parents are by and large powerless. Meanwhile, elected officials, even when faced with the economic realities of too many 4-year college students and too few jobs, take the high ground and sidestep the problem. Also, for many individuals employed in primary or secondary higher education markets, ensuring a steady stream of students is essential for job security. Finally, political realities of locally controlled public schools and conflicting community expectations prevent high school educators from actively raising concerns about the appropriateness of student high school course-taking decisions, let alone postsecondary plans; it is just easier to look the other way.

These political realities make the creation of *other ways to win* more of a challenge but in no way diminish the need. In the *one way to win* game, most lose. The first losers are those who, early in their high school years, see college as an impossible reach. Unaware of alternatives that may be equally valued by teachers or the community, they give up, drop out, or stay in school but tune out. The second losers are those who go to college unprepared, end up in remedial courses, and slowly cool out of the system and never graduate. The final losers are those who actually persist, only to discover that few jobs are available in their major; these people typically end up underemployed. Most of the losers are from the academic middle. Although assuredly some from the academic middle do graduate and do find commensurate college-level work, they are the minority; the majority would have benefited from alternatives, from *other ways to win*. In Part 3 of this book, we discuss ways to restructure the high school curriculum and high school guidance and placement services to provide these alternatives. We begin in Chapter 7 by outlining an economic rationale for alternatives that can be used to persuade the public—particularly students and parents—that there are *other ways to win*.

III
Creating *Other Ways to Win*

7

The High Skill/
High Wage Rationale

*[It is] just possible we have a surplus of graduates and a scarcity of [youth]
with real skills.*

R. Samuelson (1992, p. 75)[1]

Reverse transfers comprise one of the fastest growing groups of students in higher education. A *reverse transfer* is a student who is working on or already holds a 4-year or graduate degree but still decides to matriculate in a 2-year associate degree program—even a 1-year certificate program—at a community college. National data are not available in this area, but some 2-year postsecondary institutions report that, in certain programs, reverse transfers represent the majority of their students. On speaking tours the authors have made around the nation, some community college administrators have told us that up to 34% of their students have at least a college degree before enrolling in 2-year associate degree technical programs.

Why would anyone with a bachelor's or advanced degree invest additional time and money in a lesser degree when doing so seems illogical? One clue can be gained by noting the specific technical programs that 2-year-program reverse transfers enroll in, for example, occupation-specific technical programs in fields such as medical technologies, information technology, and automated manufacturing.

These students have discovered, albeit a bit late, that there are *other ways to win*. They have learned from experience that 4 or more years of college do not necessarily lead to a high-paying career but that an associate degree or even a 1-year certificate program can if it is in a technical field. These college graduates have learned an all-important labor market fact the hard way: Earning high wages is a result of having occupational skills that are in demand, not of education per se. This relationship between skills and wages is the concept implied by the term *high skill/high wage* work. The skills required in many high skill/high wage occupations can be learned in associate degree programs in the technologies. They can also be gained in workplace programs such as apprenticeship programs in the skilled crafts. This high skill/high wage rationale forms the economic basis for the creation of alternatives or *other ways to win* for high school graduates.

The purpose of this chapter is to explain the high skill/high wage rationale for creating alternatives for high school graduates who make up the academic middle. Our intention is to provide a rationale that can, in turn, be effectively communicated to students and parents. This chapter begins with an examination of five economic misconceptions held by students, parents, and educators that have led them to conclude there is only *one way to win*. Those who seek to promote alternatives must understand these misconceptions if they hope to argue for reasonable consideration of *other ways to win*.

SECTION I

Five Misconceptions
About the Future Labor Market

Historically, the pressure to go to college has been fueled in the United States by issues of status and class. The relatively recent explosion of high school graduates seeking 4-year college degrees can be traced to economic uncertainty, particularly as it pertains to future occupational opportunities. Most people who press youth to go to 4-year colleges have good intentions and do so for what they think are sound economic reasons. To a certain degree, however, these beliefs are based on misconceptions or misinformation about future labor market opportunities. These misconceptions were listed in Chapter

2, but we return to them now for a more detailed discussion because those who seek to create *other ways to win* need to understand them if they hope to convince others of the merit of alternatives they may develop and recommend.

> **Misconception 1**: In the future, most jobs will require a 4-year college degree.
> **Fact**: Of 5 million projected job openings annually from 1996 to 2006, only 24% will require a 4-year degree or higher.

There is a widespread misconception that in the future most jobs will require a college degree. This stems partly from general confusion about the fastest growing occupations and those that will generate the greatest number of jobs. Although the number of jobs requiring a college degree will increase more quickly than the number that will not (39% versus 16%), the fact is that in the foreseeable future for every job that requires a college degree, four will not (Shelley, 1992). Fifty-two percent of openings will require only a short to moderate on-the-job training period (Silvestri, 1997). To a certain extent, however, this may be a moot point. Most parents and students will argue that, whereas most jobs will not require a college degree, all high-paying occupations will.

> **Misconception 2**: Most high-wage jobs in the future will be in technical fields that require a college degree.
> **Fact**: The largest and fastest growing segment of the emerging technical workforce is occupations that do not require a 4-year college degree.

Most labor market experts agree that the most promising segment of the future workforce is composed of technical workers. According to an article about this new "worker elite" in *Fortune*, since 1950 the number of technical workers has increased 300% and, by 2005, will represent one fifth of all employment (Richman, 1994). There is little doubt that, aside from the traditional high-wage managerial/professional professions, the best opportunities for the future will be in the growing ranks of what Peter Drucker (1994) calls "knowledge workers," or "gold-collar" workers. The public, however, has jumped to the conclusion that 4-year college training will be required for these jobs. Not so.

Figure 7.1. The Technical Workforce

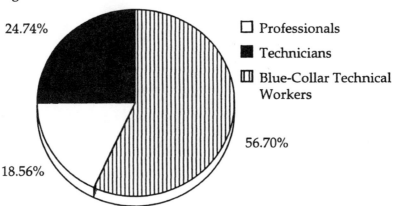

24.74%

☐ Professionals

■ Technicians

▥ Blue-Collar Technical
  Workers

56.70%

18.56%

SOURCE: Compiled from Carnevale, A., Gainer, L., & Meltzer, A. (1990).

As illustrated in Figure 7.1, the largest segment of technical workers is blue-collar or gold-collar technical workers. Using U.S. Department of Labor terms, these are primarily workers who are technicians, or are employed in the crafts, precision metal, and specialized repair occupations. These jobs do require special skills and, in some cases, they are best learned at the associate degree level, but they do not require a baccalaureate degree. In fact, among technical occupations, those that require a 4-year college degree are the fewest in number and on a percentage basis, the slowest growing (Carnevale, Gainer, & Meltzer, 1990). However, for seeking *other ways to win*, the percentage of the technical workforce that requires some postsecondary education—but at the prebaccalaureate level—is growing. For example, when applying for employment in the information technology industry, it is now more important to have relevant technical certificates than degrees. Thus, for this generation, many *other ways to win* do require postsecondary education or training, but below the 4-year level.

> **Misconception 3:** Because 4-year college graduates earn more than those with less education, a 4-year degree guarantees above-average earnings.

Fact: In the labor market, above-average wages are a return for occupational skills in demand, not education per se.

The widely held first two misconceptions, discussed previously, have in turn led to the seemingly universal faith that more education will guarantee high future earnings. Yet this is in reality a classic case of ex post facto thinking or the confusing of correlation with causation. Although education and earnings are correlated, in fact high wage rates are paid in the labor market as a premium for specialized skills in demand. This explains why some occupations that do not require a 4-year college degree, such as electrician, specialized health technicians, manufacturing technicians, and many information technology occupations, pay more than many occupations requiring the degree. It also explains what is meant by the term, *high skill/high wage occupations.*

The reason that wages and higher education are highly correlated is that in many high-paying occupations, the prerequisite skills are learned in a 4-year college program. But this is certainly not the case for all high-paying occupations. Whereas the best source of future high skill/high wage work will be the growing technical workforce, most of these occupations do not require a 4-year college degree. The skills for these jobs can be learned in postsecondary prebaccalaureate certificate and associate degree programs, formal apprenticeship programs, the military, and high school vocational education programs. The key is obtaining occupational skill.

Misconception 4: The total labor force demand for college graduates is sufficient to ensure commensurate employment for all that receive a 4-year college degree.
Fact: The U.S. Bureau of Labor forecasts that, through the year 2006, 43% of 4-year college graduates will go underemployed annually.

In light of the rapid growth in 4-year college enrollments by graduating high school seniors, one must conclude that they, their parents, and everyone else who advises them are making one optimistic assumption. Everyone seems to assume that the economy will generate increasing amounts of college-level employment to accommodate the increasing percentages of young adults earning a college degree. Unfortunately, this is not true.

According to U.S. Bureau of Labor forecasts, through the year 2006, 4-year colleges will graduate 533,000 more students than the economy will generate in commensurate employment. This suggests that there are already millions of 4-year-degree holders who are underemployed, and the numbers are likely to grow through the next century. And these are conservative estimates. Among other things, they do not take into account legal and illegal immigration into the United States by 4-year college graduates from abroad. Nor do they take into account that in the future some of this work will be done on-line by college graduates who live in other countries. Thus, the actual domestic supply of college graduates probably exceeds the demand for their services to an even greater extent than is conveyed by Bureau of Labor projections.

Even these facts, however, do not seem to persuade students or parents. While recognizing that there will be a future glut of 4-year college graduates, they have nevertheless concluded that this over-supply of college graduates is an even greater reason to get a 4-year degree. They reason that because in the future a 4-year college degree could become as common as a high school diploma is today, this degree will be required for most jobs.

> **Misconception 5:** In light of the oversupply of 4-year college graduates, this group will displace nondegree holders in good jobs that do not require a college degree.
>
> **Fact:** Surveys of employers have not revealed that they prefer college graduates for jobs that do not require a degree. More important, 4-year college graduates will not displace nondegree holders who have specialized occupational skills in demand.

This last myth is the pivotal fear that fuels the mania for a 4-year college degree. Many parents and students worry that an increase in the number of 4-year-degree holders will result in a situation where those without a bachelor's will not be able to compete even for jobs that do not require a college education. There is evidence that this fear is not well founded. In a national survey of employers in the 13 largest industrial sectors, "10 of 13 industry groups ranked the need for vocational training higher than the need for a college degree" (Stern, 1992, p. 25), confirming the importance of skill, not degrees, in the hiring decisions made by firms.

Nonetheless, there will undoubtedly be cases of 4-year-degree holders pushing out high school graduates in some low skill/low wage work, particularly in retailing, food service, and recreation. In the competition for technical high skill/high wage occupations, however, 4-year college graduates will not displace high school graduates or associate degree graduates who have the required prerequisite skills. A person with a 4-year degree in psychology, for example, is not going to displace an individual with an information technology occupational certificate, or an associate degree in a technical area.

Furthermore, the logic of pursuing a 4-year college degree because it may lead to a labor market advantage in competing for low skill/low wage work makes little sense, dollar-wise. A 4-year college degree can cost from $50,000 to $120,000. Add the interest costs from student loans and forgone earnings while in college and this situation makes even less sense. Economist Lester Thurow (1996) points out that, in general, the return on investment for a 4-year college degree is so low that no corporation would invest money in such a venture. The hard reality is that a growing number of college-degree holders will never see a positive return on their higher education investment, meaning that they will never get a job that allows them to recoup their higher education investment. The secret to getting into high-paying occupations for this generation is to gain occupational skills in demand—not education per se.

SECTION II

The High Skill/High Wage Rationale
for Creating *Other Ways to Win*

If the goal of students is future economic security, the focus of their postsecondary planning should be on obtaining job skills that prepare them to compete for a limited supply of high skill/high wage work. This focus differs significantly from that of getting a 4-year college degree on the basis of the naive faith that it will lead to a good job. This advice is particularly suited for high school graduates from the academic middle of their graduating class because odds are that they will not be among those who ultimately will find a college-level job even if they do graduate. Despair is not the appropriate emotion, however; there are *other ways to win*. As pointed out in a recent U.S. Department of Labor publication, "Workers with less education, but who are employed in jobs that require special skills or training, earn as much as [4-year] college graduates who do not re-quire [skills] training to get their jobs" (Eck, 1993, p. 37).

The message for academically average students is that they should consider, from among the high skill/high wage occupations, those for which the job prospects are good and the prerequisite skills can be learned at the postsecondary, 2-year technical degree level or in work-based training programs. They should also develop a career plan that enables them to learn the skills needed to compete for these occupations. Examples of such occupations follow.

Examples of Prebaccalaureate
High Skill/High Wage Occupations

The best way for academically average students to win in the fierce competition for above-average-paying jobs in the future is to focus on getting the skills needed to compete for high skill/high wage occupations that require something less than a 4-year college degree. Table 7.1 lists some of these occupations according to broad industry categories.

This list is by no means complete; even within these limited oc-cupation titles, there are thousands of individual job titles for each occupation. All of these occupations pay yearly earnings above the national average. The key to obtaining these jobs and earnings is oc-cupational skills. For example, whereas an untrained short-order cook earns minimum wage, a professionally trained chef from one of the recognized culinary institutes earns a higher starting wage than a schoolteacher. If the chef is even moderately successful, he or she will always outearn public school teachers—and the majority of college professors as well.

Of course, money and the status of going on to postsecondary education is not everything. Aside from monetary rewards from jobs, most individuals also seek and are the most successful in ca-reers that are consistent with their interests, talents, and perceptions of themselves. As indicated by this list, prebaccalaureate high skill/high wage work can appeal to all types of individual interests and preferences. There are occupational choices for those who want to help people, who like to work outdoors, who like to take things

TABLE 7.1   Worker Elite High-Skill/High-Wage Occupations
Not Requiring a Baccalaureate Degree

Craft and Construction

Construction drafting

Construction project manager

Heating/air-conditioning
technician

Plumbing/pipe-fitting
technician

Precision welding

Specialized carpentry and
installation

Specialized interior finishing and
installation

Health Occupations

Dental assistant

Dental hygienist

Emergency medical technician

Home health aide

Licensed practical nurse

Medical laboratory technician

Medical record technician

Optometric technician

Radiology technician

Surgical technologist

Manufacturing

Computer-controlled equipment
operator

Drafting technician

Electronics engineering
technician

Electronics lab technician

Engineering technician

Manufacturing systems operator

Manufacturing technician

Service Occupations

Accountant

Agribusiness sales

Automatic office manager

Commercial design

Computer graphics corrections

Criminal justice and corrections

Data processing manager

Firefighter

Law enforcement/protection
occupations

Library technician

Paralegal

Professionally trained chef

Specialty auto mechanic

**Technical Service, Repair, and
Installation**

Airframe mechanic

Avionics repair technician

Biomedical equipment
technician

Electromechanical repair
technician

Information Technology

Computer systems installation
and repair

Computer systems specialist

Software support specialist

Telecommunications installation
and repair

TABLE 7.2 High-Skill/High-Wage Occupations in Construction/Manufacturing

Occupational Group	*Craftsperson* *Blue-Collar Technical*	*Technician*	*Professional Technical*	
			4-year degree	Graduate School
Preparation Required	High school vocational education Apprenticeships 1-year technical certificate	2-year associate degree	4-year degree	Graduate School
Typical Job Function	Testing Service Maintenance Routine analysis Repair Assemble Operate Construct	Manufacturing Production Operations Quality assurance Technical sales Maintenance	Complex design Product development Testing and evaluation Routine design	Basic research Research development Theoretical analysis
Representative Job Titles	Electrician Factory assembler Tester Machinist Operator Computer operator Mechanic	Engineer's aide Service technician Drafter Foreman Programmer Inspector System analyst Technical sales/services Project manager Technical operations manager Customer service representative Field operations supervisor Data communications manager Surveyor	Design engineer Systems engineer Product development supervisor Plant manager Engineer	Research scientist Engineer Mathematician Physicist Professor

apart, who are artistically creative, who want to work on the East Coast or the West Coast, and who want to dress professionally each day (or not). The choices are endless.

How does one learn the prerequisite skills required in the high skill/high wage occupations? They are learned in a variety of settings. Table 7.2, for example, portrays the occupational structure in the construction and manufacturing fields. Some occupations, particularly in construction crafts, can actually be learned in high school vocational education programs. Still others can be learned in formal work-based training programs, such as apprenticeships organized by employer and employee groups. Most, however, require either 1- or 2-year postsecondary educational training; if they do not require it, having postsecondary training results in a labor market advantage in competing for jobs.

This latter point is important: A majority of today's high school students and their parents have decided that their only option is to attend a higher education institution after graduation, and currently their preference is a 4-year college education. Although they may be open to alternatives to a 4-year college degree, it is unlikely they will be receptive to plans that do not include some type of postsecondary education. Because many high skill/high wage occupations require postsecondary education—but at the prebaccalaureate level—those in the academic middle can both go on to higher education and prepare for occupations in which their chance for success is good. Furthermore, many such 2-year postsecondary technical programs articulate with 4-year baccalaureate programs and thus provide an opportunity for those who do well at the 2-year postsecondary level to proceed with further academic study, if they choose.

What about future employment prospects? Compared with the outlook for 4-year college degree graduates, the employment outlook for those preparing for high skill/high wage work requiring less than a 4-year (prebaccalaureate) degree is great!

Occupational Outlook for
High Skill/High Wage Occupations
Not Requiring a Baccalaureate Degree

The occupational and earnings outlook for most high skill/high wage occupations that require less than a baccalaureate degree is

TABLE 7.3 Occupational Groups Ranked by Earnings, Net
Openings, Percentage Female, and Required Training

	Earnings	Net Openings	% Female	Required Training
Managerial/ professional	1	6	47	1
Craft, precision metal, specialized repair	2	3	9	2
Technical support	3	1	64	3
Service	4	4	25	5
Operative, laborer	5	2	60	4
Farming, fishing	6	5	16	6

SOURCES: Data compiled from Eck, A. (1993).

generally good. To begin with, technical or information workers are projected to comprise one fifth of all workers by 2005. Most of these occupations do not require a 4-year college degree but do require prerequisite skills; thus, those not having a 4-year college degree but who do have relevant skills will not be in danger of being displaced by unskilled baccalaureate degree holders. Meanwhile, the earnings of those holding prebaccalaureate high skill/high wage jobs will compare favorably with most college graduates and will exceed those of many. These statements are supported by the labor market data summarized in Table 7.3.

Table 7.3 contains important information for those who seek to alert students from the academic middle, their parents, and faculty that there are *other ways to win* besides a 4-year college degree. In the first column of the table are listed six broad occupational clusters used by the U.S. Bureau of the Census when collecting monthly employment and wage data.

The second column of Table 7.3 ranks the occupational groups from highest to lowest according to the average annual salary of individuals who work in occupations contained in each cluster. The highest-earning group is managerial/professional, which includes such occupations as lawyers, doctors, accountants, and schoolteachers. This ranking is probably not a surprise and actually lies behind the *one way to win* paradigm. But wait. What is the second highest-paying group? It is craft, precision metal, and specialized repair; this category includes, for example, those in the building trade occupations, manufacturing systems technicians, and electromechanical repair specialists. And notice the third highest-paying occupational group—technicians, which includes medical lab techs, electronics lab techs, electronics engineering techs, and so forth.

Many high skill/high wage occupations that do not require a BA degree can be found in all six clusters—agribusiness, for example, employs thousands of technical workers—but the largest percentages of these occupations are found in the craft/precision metal/repair and technical support clusters. This concentration of high skill/high wage occupations that do not require a BA degree in the second and third highest-paying occupational clusters provides the fundamental rationale for creating *other ways to win*. Specifically, it explains the following reality:

On average, the yearly income of individuals employed in the craft/precision metal/repair areas and as technicians will be higher than that for all college graduates except those who find work in the managerial/professional ranks.

The importance of this labor market reality is magnified by considering the occupational opportunity outlook in these clusters that is summarized in the third column of Table 7.3. In this column, the six occupational groups are rank-ordered according to net (demand minus supply) job opportunities. Now a more complex and revealing picture unfolds. Although managerial/professional is the highest-paying cluster, it ranks last in terms of opportunity; in fact, in many occupations, the demand for workers is half that of the yearly supply of new job seekers. For example, each year, colleges graduate

58,000 students with degrees in accounting for only 38,000 projected jobs. Although the public thinks there is a shortage of engineers, there is a worldwide glut; in the United States alone, colleges graduate 85,000 engineers yearly for 52,000 jobs (see Table 5.2).

Meanwhile, notice that the second and third highest-paying occupational group—craft/precision metal/repair and technical support—are also third and first, respectively, in projected job opportunities. In many occupations within these two occupational clusters, wages are high and the number of job openings greatly exceeds the number of individuals training for these jobs. For example, in the craft/precision metal/repair cluster, training programs prepare annually only 133,000 workers for 455,000 high skill/high wage jobs. Opportunities in this category are tremendous and often are overlooked because, relative to other occupational groups, its size is small and actually getting smaller. This decline in numbers, however, reflects the growing technical nature of the workplace that requires fewer workers but a higher skill level for those who remain. It is important that the rising skill level of those jobs that remain has resulted in increasing wages. It is not uncommon for a cross-skilled electrician in technical manufacturing to earn $80,000 a year with 4 weeks of vacation and job offers that would make most lawyers envious.

Opportunities for
Special Populations

In Chapter 3, it was argued that, although it is a matter of national pride that those who can benefit from a 4-year college program be able to do so regardless of socioeconomic background or gender, special populations may well be the most hurt by the existence of a single alternative—a 4-year college degree—and therefore would benefit the most from socially acceptable and economically viable alternatives. The fourth column of Table 7.3 illustrates this point in more concrete terms. It shows the percentage of women in the workforce in each occupational cluster. Women have just about gained parity in the highest-paying occupational group, namely, managerial/ professional. As a result, the competition among college graduates of both genders for the few jobs in the professional ranks should get even fiercer. But notice the percentage of women in the second highest-paying group, craft/precision metal/specialized repair. Only 9% of that workforce are women. The numbers for minorities are similar. Although the growth in the ranks of women and minorities who are chief executives receives most of the press, the real problem is that, aside from health occupations, too few of either are among the ranks of technical workers.

Importance of Occupational Skill and Postsecondary Technical Education

The final column of Table 7.3 confirms the high skill/high wage rationale for the creation of *other ways to win,* specifically, the argument that the objective of postsecondary education is to acquire the skills required to obtain high skill/high wage work, not just a degree per se, and that high wages are a return for these skills. In the fifth column, the occupational clusters are ranked from highest to lowest by percentage of workers who reported to the U.S. Bureau of the Census that their job requires some degree of formal training. If skills, not education, are the key to high wages, one would expect the rank ordering of the six occupational groups according to earnings and the percentage of workers reporting that their job requires prerequisite skills to be the same. This is exactly what was found for the three highest-paying occupational groups. Importantly, only in the managerial/professional group are these skills learned primarily at the 4-year college degree level; in the other two categories, the majority of occupations are best prepared for at the 1- and 2-year postsecondary level (see Table 7.1) or in formal on-the-job training programs such as apprenticeships.

The high skill/high wage rationale mentioned above provides a strong argument that *other ways to win* do not require a 4-year college degree. This is the rationale behind creating alternatives for those in the academic middle. Understanding this rationale is critical for those who seek to create alternatives. It is even more critical that the rationale be effectively communicated to parents and students. Thus, we conclude this chapter by suggesting five points to present to parents.

Five Points to Make
With Parents

Those who seek to create alternatives for students in the academic middle need to know why pursuing a 4-year college degree is not a sound plan for many students and what alternative labor market opportunities exist. Ultimately, however, high school students, their parents, and even many educators must be convinced. To assist in this mission to dispel the *one way to win* myth, the following five points should be considered before deciding on a 4-year degree program.

Five Things to Consider Before
Deciding to Pursue a 4-Year College Degree

Point 1. Because of open admissions, getting into college is relatively easy, whereas graduating is not. Only about half who matriculate ever graduate in 6 years.

Point 2. In the decade ahead, the number of 4-year college graduates will far exceed commensurate job opportunities.

Point 3. Technical workers are the fastest-growing and economically most promising segment of the labor force.

Point 4. The largest number and fastest-growing group of jobs among technical workers can be trained for at the 2-year associate degree level.

Point 5. On average, technical workers without a 4-year college degree will earn higher salaries than all 4-year college graduates except those who find work in the professional ranks.

The point to be made in offering these arguments to students and parents is that, although the decision to attend a 4-year college is theirs, they should understand that (a) they face high odds, particularly when one graduates from high school with poor academic credentials and (b) there are alternatives. The issue of higher education costs was not included in this argument, but some of you may wish to add it. Data regarding the magnitude of the average student loan debt typically acquired by those pursuing a baccalaureate degree can be a real wake-up call. Thus, some people may wish to add this dimension to the argument; others may think that discussion of money is a private matter. Ultimately, each person must tailor this argument and data to meet his or her circumstances.

Other Ways to Win

The dramatic increase in 4-year college attendance by graduating high school seniors can be traced to genuine economic uncertainty about the future employment outlook. This uncertainty has led to the "anxious class"; this anxiety has led to the conclusion that the best bet is a 4-year degree. In previous chapters, we explored the harm done by this one-sided advice. In this chapter, economic labor market data have been presented that demonstrate the presence of a good alternative, namely, 2-year technical education that will lead to high skill/high wage careers in the ranks of the new technocrats.

The message to students, parents, and teachers is that, on the basis of the five points outlined here, there are *other ways to win*. Although going to a 4-year college in preparation for the professions is a very good postsecondary plan for some students, is it a realistic plan for all? A good alternative for those who want to go on to higher education, particularly for those from the academic middle as indicated by their high school academic performance, is 2-year technical education in preparation for competing for high skill/high wage work.

Persuading students and parents that something less than a 4-year degree is worth considering will not be an easy sell. It will require significant counseling and career planning involving both parents and students. This guidance is the topic of Chapter 8.

Note

1. R. Samuelson, August 31, 1992, p. 75. Copyright © 1992, Newsweek, Inc. All rights reserved. Reprinted by permission.

8

Step 1
Providing Systematic Career Guidance for Students and Structured Feedback for Parents

A parent's understanding is an incredible gift.

D. Muse

The fundamental challenge for those who would promote *other ways to win* is to help students and their parents make more informed secondary and postsecondary academic decisions. Many, if not most, who pursue the *one way to win* strategy make no conscious decision to do so; for them, pursuing a 4-year degree is a default action. Rather than facing reality—which for many is not as pleasant as ignoring it—and making appropriate secondary and postsecondary choices, they take the easy way out. They do what everyone else does. Much the same thing can be said for the course they select in high school. Most drift around in the so-called college prep program of study.

A widely held misconception in U.S. high schools is that students are tracked into a regimented set of courses that limits their options. In fact, the opposite is more often the case. Whereas in the 1950s and 1960s, students had to complete a structured program of study to graduate from high school, today they need only accumulate a specified number of credits in broad content areas. The bottom line: Students can take nearly any course they or their parents choose. The implication of this trend is that the success of creating *other ways to win* depends primarily on parents' and students' decisions that these alternatives are worth enrolling in. The most sophisticated and well-intended efforts to provide students from the academic middle with more realistic postsecondary alternatives will fail if students and their parents do not buy the concept and elect the appropriate programs of study.

Nor should one underestimate the difficulty of convincing these clients of the public school system that there is value in anything less than the traditional college prep program of study and pursuit of a 4-year degree. Aside from the genuine parental concern for the economic future of children and from the social pressure to go to college, a well-financed higher education primary and secondary industry has a vested interest in maintaining the conventional wisdom of *one way to win* in order to maintain the enrollments at baccalaureate colleges.

For these reasons, the first step in creating *other ways to win* is to foster more informed decision making by teens and their parents by providing (a) a systematic career development/guidance program and (b) a means of getting feedback to parents regarding their teens' readiness to pursue postsecondary education. These two activities are discussed in this chapter.

SECTION I

Systematic Career Guidance
for All Students

The need for better career guidance for youth is highlighted in many data sources that are easily found. Although 68.8% of all graduating female high school students expect to be working in the professions by age 30, most probably have not thought seriously about career plans. In the Class of 1998 Follow-Up Study (Gray & Xiaoli, 1999), for example, most students indicated that they wished they had more opportunities to explore careers. Important for this discussion, of the three academic groupings identified in the study, those who graduated with the poorest academic credentials were the most likely to wish they had had more career guidance.

Supporting the argument for the need of more career development/guidance is a 1999 national survey (Shell Poll, 1999) of high school students. To begin with, the *one way to win* conventional wisdom was well entrenched; 81% indicated they plan to continue their education, and 79% expected to go to a 4-year college. Yet only 50% indicated they feel confident about their choices, even though 84% said they had given some serious thought to the topic. Meanwhile, 40% said they had not received adequate career guidance, and 30% indicated they had not had much help selecting courses in high school. These findings suggest an inconsistency. Whereas most plan to pursue the *one way to win* strategy—and other studies indicated most are doing so to "get a better job,"—only about half are at all sure about what their career goals are. The problem is that the latter (career focus) predicts success in the former (going to college and getting a college-level job).

Career Choices and
Postsecondary Success

There are good reasons for all students and parents to support better career development/guidance programs independent of academic talent. Of the four most important indicators of postsecondary persistence (academic skills, money, involvement, and commitment), it is the last, commitment, that is the most important. As argued in *Getting Real: Helping Teens Find Their Future* (Gray, 2000), if we are to move beyond just counting how many go to college and begin to take responsibility for how they do once they get there, then career development/guidance becomes as important as college prep academics.

Students do not flunk out of college anymore. It is almost impossible to flunk out; they just leave. The first group leaves during the first six weeks of the freshman year, which accounts for 30% of the 30% that fail to complete their freshman year. Others wait until they must declare a major at the end of the sophomore year. Because upwards of 70% of incoming freshmen indicate that they are not sure what they will major in, it is not surprising that having done little to clarify their goals in two years, many leave at the end of the sophomore year. Still others practice "academic major of the month," changing majors frequently. Although changing an academic major once may be healthy, multiple changes are not. Many who do so make the final choice—not because after 4 or 5 years of college they have finally found their vocation, but because it is a major that allows them to at least graduate. Not surprisingly, when they do graduate, most end up underemployed.

Thus, perhaps the number one argument for career development/systematic guidance programs is that they are important for all students: both the academically blessed and the less blessed. Most students are in higher education for labor market advantage in competing for well-paying and satisfying jobs. Those who go to college, be it for 1, 2, or 4 years, with some clarity as to which career they want to pursue, are most likely to succeed.

Systematic Career
Guidance Defined

Contemporary views of career guidance suggest that it is more than a set of activities and services; it is a systematic program aimed at a specific outcome. The outcome at the junior and senior high school levels is the development of a level of individual career maturity that will lead to realistic high school academic course selection; such selection, in turn, will increase the probability that each student, especially those in the academic middle, will make a successful transition from high school to postsecondary education or a career. Career guidance should be coordinated and coherent in its responsibilities to students and parents. More about this topic is discussed in Section II of this chapter.

The principal emphasis in career guidance at the high school level should be on secondary and postsecondary academic and career planning. Such planning should begin by elevating the readiness of adolescents to participate in life as independent, goal-directed persons and then move on to aiding in tentative career choices. These choices are to be confirmed or modified by academic performance and changing preferences as a student progresses through high school. The point is that career guidance program activities in the senior high school must take each student from where he or she is in coping with developmental tasks integral to career development and lead that person to create a specific set of preferences and plans for achieving those goals (which is the substance of the individual career plan discussed in the following).

Within a systematic career guidance program are myriad activities that can facilitate career maturity that, in turn, will lead to realistic high school course selection and postsecondary plans. One listing of such career guidance activities of particular relevance to the focus of this book has been advanced by Chew (1993). They include, in abridged form, the following:

1. Counselors and school districts should implement a comprehensive developmental guidance model for K-12 students, emphasizing technical careers within the career component.
2. Counselors should provide all students with interest and aptitude assessments (beginning not later than the eighth grade) to help them plan postsecondary education goals.
3. Counselors should provide schoolwide activities that promote the awareness of technical career opportunities.
4. Counselors should provide students with information about community or technical colleges.
5. Counselors should give attention to women and minorities by providing them with information regarding unique opportunities for them in technical careers.
6. Counselors should assist special needs students (e.g., learning disabled, physically disabled, teen parents, and economically disadvantaged) in making transitions from secondary to postsecondary education.
7. Counselors must have access to appropriate materials and resources that explain the options of tech-prep and technical careers.
8. Counselors should help students develop a portfolio that summarizes their credentials, both educational and experiential. (pp. 32-35)

For a complete discussion of other alternatives, consult Herr and Cramer's *Career Guidance and Counseling Through the Life Span* (1996). We chose here to emphasize what should be the heart of a systematic career guidance program for all students: the individual career plan

TABLE 8.1 Career Maturity Through Young Adulthood

		Approximate Ages		
Preschool	*5-9*	*10-14*	*15-18*	*19+*
Formulation of self-concept ⟶		Translation into postsecondary plan ⟶		
Developing preferences ⟶			Choice ⟶	Transition
Fantasy ⟶		Tentative ⟶		Realistic

SOURCE: Roe, A. (1954).

(ICP). Before we discuss the ICP, it is important that the reader understand the concept of career maturity, the development of which is the goal of an ICP.

The Problem of
Adolescent Career Immaturity

One very important aspect of individual development is *career development*, the lifelong process of decisions and actions taken to decide on, prepare for, enter into, and be successful in an occupation or occupations. Psychologists and vocational guidance specialists have studied career development and have constructed a model of the typical career development phases of youth (Herr & Cramer, 1996, p. 308). This model is presented in Table 8.1.

Notice that each phase is associated with a typical chronological age. An individual exhibiting signs of "mature" career development will be learning about and acquiring the self-assessment and career-planning skills relevant to the phase of career development appropriate for his or her age. According to the model, a mature individual should have moved from fantasy in the elementary grades to realism at the time of graduation from high school—realism in terms of having made a tentative decision to prepare to enter a particular field of work. Importantly, this decision, though tentative, is mature to the degree to which it is based on a realistic assessment of skills and/or preparation at the time of high school graduation, as well as on projected labor force opportunities. When roughly 70% of all female high school graduates and 50% of all male graduates indicate they expect to work in the professions, one can make a strong argument that massive career immaturity (see Hoyt, 1994) is afoot in U.S. high schools. Understanding the thought process that leads to this massive fantasy is critical to planning efforts to improve the career maturity of those in the academic middle. In this case, psychological decision-making theories are useful.

Career development theories are best thought of as theories about how individuals make decisions—in this case, decisions about what type of work they will prepare for and engage in. Several of the major theories are predicated on the assumption that persons can make logical decisions based on the availability of information and help from counselors or other professionals to assist them in weighing and evaluating their alternatives. Decision theories are also based on economics; they hold that any choice will maximize gain and minimize loss in aspects that are the most important to the particular individual (e.g., income, prestige, security) (Herr & Cramer, 1996, p. 185).

Some theories, such as Holland's (1985), are optimistic, democratic, and therefore intuitively pleasing. Such characteristics suggest that career decisions are "an expression of personality and not a random event. Individuals choose an occupation that is consistent with an individual's personality or self-concept" (p. 219). Yet, this construct seems inadequate for explaining the current situation; almost two thirds of high school students are making the same postsecondary choice—namely, attending a 4-year college to gain entry into the professional occupations—but certainly they cannot all have the same abilities or personalities.

A theory is needed that explains a seeming suppression of individual differences, one that explains irrational acts and bad decisions or indecision. Cognitive dissonance theory seems to best explain the present state of affairs. Individuals faced with either too much, too little, or conflicting information make decisions intended to reduce the personal anxiety created by this overload; in this case, they decide to go to college. As suggested by Herr and Cramer (1992),

The magnitude of information and the number of factors to be considered in decision making are so great that the individual chooses prematurely, without fully considering the implications of the choice, in order to reduce the besieging pressures as the torrents of information relevant to the choice are sorted out. The person then reinforces the choice by rationalization: selective attention to those data making the choice appear satisfying to self and to external observers. Although the chooser "knows" there are other options and better ones, particularly over the longer range, it is comforting to make a selection and suppress the costs of its unrealism. (p. 177)

This thesis clearly describes the present situation. One key phrase is "external observers." For example, Jepsen (1989) speculates that, in adolescence, most career decisions are made in response to a social context. He argues that adolescents are greatly influenced by various reference groups, such as parents, teachers, and friends. These groups send overt and/or subtle messages regarding their expectations. Adolescents respond to these expectations, sometimes referred to as peer or parental pressure, in overt and covert ways. In short, they say and do one thing but think another. They do what conforms to social expectations—in this case, they go to college and express an intent to enter the professions—even though they covertly or privately know it is the wrong decision.

Gelatt (1989, p. 253) suggests that this is all normal under the circumstances. In what must be identified as a classic positive spin, he calls this situation "positive uncertainty," a healthy response to an unknown future caused by ambiguous and conflicting information. In Gelatt's model, the *one way to win* mentality is natural. It may well be understandable, given that no viable alternatives are provided, but it is also terribly costly for all except underenrolled 4-year colleges and universities. It is especially costly to those in the academic middle, where the losers in the *one way to win* game greatly outnumber winners, even among those few who actually persist in their quest for a baccalaureate degree. Thus, the first goal of efforts to create alternatives for those in the academic middle is to replace "positive uncertainty" with "tentative certainty" among high school youth through systematic career guidance. The key element in this program is the ICP.

Student Outcome Objectives for Career Development/ Guidance Programs

In order for students to opt for *other ways to win* they must have a career reason to do so. Developing such a motive is the objective of career development/guidance programs. Often these programs suffer from clear direction as to which student outcomes are desired. To be specific, we recommend three (Gray, 2000).

1. By the 10th grade, all students will have participated in activities designed to help them identify several tentative career interests to prepare for after high school.
2. In the 11th and 12th grades, all students will participate in activities that allow them to verify or reject these choices, using the results to develop postsecondary plans.
3. All students will graduate with a postsecondary plan that has a high probability of success, and which will enable them to realize their hopes and dreams.

Systematic career development/guidance programs are composed of a sequential series of activities aimed at developing a student's career maturity. Ideally, such efforts start in the primary grades, but certainly no later than the middle school level. The goal is that by the 10th grade, students will have identified several related career interests. It will be quite natural for teens in the 10th grade to have several—even many—career interests. The point is that by the 10th grade, they should be related. A student who is considering building construction or automated machining is on the right track, whereas a student who is still stuck on professional basketball or tattoo artist is not.

The 10th grade is important because it is a decision-making point in the high school curriculum. Students should choose high school academic courses for the junior and senior year based on their postsecondary plan and that plan, in turn, should be based on tentative career choices. Thus, career development/guidance activities for K-10 students should be focused on fostering tentative career choices by the 10th grade.

The 11th and 12th grades are the years when students should be helped to verify and narrow the related career interests they have identified by the 10th grade. Job shadowing, internships, volunteer work, and part-time employment are all excellent ways to help students verify tentative interests. Doing so is critical. Having a tentative career direction is an absolute prerequisite for success in postsecondary planning and postsecondary pursuits. This choice may change in college but, if the original choice was well thought out, the change will likely be to a related field. Thus, the goal is to have all graduates ready to implement a plan that has a high probability of success. For many, that plan will be *other ways to win.*

There are many ways to organize schools. Two specific initiatives develop the three student outcome goals listed previously. These two elements of career guidance will be discussed in detail: the individual career plans and career majors or pathways.

The Individual Career Plan

An *individual career plan* (ICP) is a process that leads to a product (the plan) that assists students and parents in relating each student's career interests and postsecondary higher education aspirations to individual aptitudes and achievements. The specific objective is to make a plan of action that the student will follow after graduation. The plan provides concrete postsecondary plans and tentative career goals, identifies the steps (e.g., courses to be taken in high school) that are required, and reinforces the commitment and responsibility of each student to take charge of his or her career. This written document is developed jointly by students, their parents, and school personnel. It becomes a part of the student's permanent record file. Thus, although ICP development is a joint venture and the postsecondary plan ultimately reflects decisions made by students and parents, the school is responsible for managing the process and for providing students and parents with objective data that enable them to periodically evaluate the feasibility of the plan. This critical issue is discussed later in the chapter.

Because there are a number of ICP models, ultimately each high school faculty member will have to select one or develop his or her own. One such model, called "Get a . . . Life" Personal Planning Portfolio, was developed by the American School Counselor Association with a grant from the National Occupational Information Coordinating Committee (NOICC). The program is systematic; it recommends certain activities at certain specific points in the K-12 years for each student. The resultant portfolio becomes part of a student's permanent record and follows him or her from one level of schooling to another. The Personal Planning Portfolio is divided into two strategic parts. The first, the personal file, contains individual reflections about tentative career plans that are gained from career guidance activities that the school system provides to all students. The second, the competency file, contains objective data that the school system provides regarding a student's academic achievements and abilities. The school expands the competency file at least once each year—usually at the end of the year—on the basis of the student's academic achievements and experiences.

Ideally, the portfolio would first be developed in the seventh or eighth grade so that it could serve as a basis for high school first-year course selection. In these early years, most plans will call for preparation for the transition to a 4-year college and plans to pursue professional work. In the seventh, eighth, and even ninth grades, this level of unreality is tolerable and perhaps even desirable. Clearly, though, the goal is to have students and parents, by the end of the 10th grade or, at the latest, the 11th grade, facing the reality that, for most students—in our estimate, 70%—the *one way to win* paradigm of a 4-year college degree and a career in the professions is not very realistic.

Once again, the goal of this model and of all others is to move students from a state of career immaturity or naive optimism to a state of career maturity or tentative certainty. This transition is achieved by structuring situations that juxtapose tentative postsecondary plans with objective data regarding academic ability and achievement. Thus, it is important that the ICP strategy chosen or developed include periodic wake-up calls or objective feedback to students and parents that facilitates the most realistic evaluation of postsecondary plans and career aspirations.

Unfortunately, since the 1960s, high school educators have grown leery of activities designed to give parents anything but good news. This attitude is understandable because, increasingly, parents either lay total blame on the school or ignore the message. Tired of hearing from parents and others about the one youth who went to college and graduated despite his counselor's assessment that he was not college material, counselors also have taken a passive role. This attitude must change. Presenting the type of data described previously to parents as part of an ICP process will help high school educators become more willing to deliver wake-up calls. After all, these data are part of an ongoing process that includes delivery of an important message: Postsecondary plans are your (parents and students) decision; our (educators) role is to provide the best education possible to achieve these plans but also to provide you with objective data regarding your probability of academic success.

Such thoughtful confrontation between plans and academic achievement is critical to the creation of *other ways to win* because it ensures that the alternative emphasis within the college prep program of study recommended in the next chapter will be considered seriously. The critical players in this thoughtful confrontation are, of course, individual students, but parents also play an important role. In fact, the successful creation of *other ways to win* relies on reaching out to parents to challenge the *one way to win* myth and to provide them with advice and counsel regarding their children's higher education plans.

Career Pathways/ Career Majors/Career Academies

A more comprehensive and ambitious effort to develop career maturity among teens involves adding career majors or pathways to the high school program of study. Typical pathways or majors include health/human services, business/marketing, science/natural resources, engineering/technical, and arts/humanities. Each student is required to choose a career major or pathway on entering high school. Making this choice is the focus of a comprehensive career development program in the preceding grades. In larger high schools with more scheduling and course options, different academic programs of study are developed for each occupational level with each major. In smaller high schools the number of majors is typically four (for example, engineering/industrial, health/science and human services, business technology, and arts/humanities). In these smaller high schools, developing many programs of study may not be realistic. Instead, they use programs such as tech prep to provide a focused academic sequence for those interested in preparing for 2-year technical education. Career majors become the focus of career verification efforts in the junior and senior years.

The most comprehensive model of education reform designed to promote academic and career maturity, and specific occupation skills is career academies. A career academy is an entirely self-contained academic unit focused on providing students the occupational skills related to a specific career cluster such as health, information technology, and so forth. Career academies are found primarily in urban centers or large districts that have multiple high schools, providing the opportunity to designate one or more a career magnet. Thus, a career academy may be a public school devoted to teaching about one career cluster. However, it is possible to establish a career academy within a large high school in much the same way large high schools have established various houses or schools within a school. In the career academy approach, the occupation cluster becomes the context for academic as well as skill building. Often career academies are sponsored directly by related industry.

Perhaps the true importance of the ICP and career majors/pathways/academies efforts is the message it sends to students and parents, namely, that career maturity and career focus are critical to success. The objective of these efforts is not to vocationalize the curriculum nor take decision making out of the hands of families, but to promote postsecondary success by helping teens and parents make better decisions.

Underlying career guidance, individual career plans, and career pathway efforts is career information. Neither students nor parents can choose what they do not know about. Information is power if it is accurate, relevant, and timely to choices that need to be made. However, if one has very limited and biased information, it reduces the likelihood that choices made will be free, informed, or reflect the comprehensive exploration and reality testing that is included in the meaning of the term *career maturity.*

SECTION II

Providing Feedback to Parents

It is unlikely that even the most sophisticated career guidance program will successfully create a modest level of career maturity among high school seniors or interest them in more realistic post-secondary educational alternatives unless it is accompanied by a parallel effort to provide counseling through objective feedback to parents on labor market realities, college costs, and their child's academic credentials. The parents' role in promoting the *one way to win* mentality was documented in Chapter 2 (see Figure 2.1). The forces behind the parental *one way to win* push are complex. They include the reality that (a) college attendance has replaced high school graduation as the final visible sign of parental effectiveness and (b) society seems to agree that once their adolescent is in college, parents have provided the most important opportunity in the society for their child and have done all they can. Parents have their children's best interests in mind when they promote 4-year college because they see it as the *only way to win.* To quote Secretary of Labor Robert Reich,

> A widening economic gap between better-educated and less skilled workers is creating an "anxious class" of Americans worried about the kind of future their children will face. These people . . . are justifiably uneasy about their own standing and fearful about their children's futures. (Naylor, 1994, p. A4)

Reich's "anxious class" probably includes parents of students in the academic middle. These parents may themselves be in jobs threatened by downsizing or technological elimination. Faced with such uncertainty, they would certainly hope to protect their children from a similar fate in the future. They read that college graduates currently earn 83% more than high school graduates over their life-times and conclude that a 4-year college degree is the only hope, the *only way to win*. Although this logic is flawed, parents can be very reluctant to endorse alternatives, or as summarized by Paul Barton (1994) of the Policy Information Center, "Parents generally fear what appears to them to be any form of tracking away from the college route" (p. 3), a point we return to in Chapters 9 and 10.

Thus, working effectively with parents rests on effective communication of the economic axioms of career planning and provision of objective data regarding outlooks for academically average students. At the same time, it means being mindful that, for many parents, anything less than a 4-year degree for their child will be very difficult to accept. In this context, when and how feedback and counseling regarding their child's developing academic credentials are provided becomes very important. Such information needs to be highly structured and the same for all parents of all high school students. Separate efforts, distinct from programs for the academically blessed, will not work.

Delivering the Wake-Up Call to Parents

Parental involvement is widely viewed as a key factor in school effectiveness (see "Amherst School," 1994). Therefore, public school educators expend considerable energy promoting parental involvement and parent groups at the elementary and middle school levels. These efforts typically diminish, however, once students get to high school. It is difficult to decide whether this withering of parental involvement is because of the belief by high school educators that parental interaction is not traditional at this level or because, over the years, parents become less inclined to be involved at the high school level and thus stop trying. There are some exceptions, however, such as the Connecticut Regional Vocational High Schools, wherein secondary schools have very active and effective parent associations. These and other success stories around the United States prove that it is possible to get high school parents more involved than is currently the practice.

Our argument is that such parental involvement is not only possible but essential to successful efforts to get those in the academic middle to consider alternatives. Parents are intimately involved in the present pressure on youth to go to a 4-year college. If students are to be receptive to alternatives, their parents must be too. The following 4-step program is recommended.

A Four-Step Parental Involvement Program

In the following four-step, or four-part, parental involvement program, the intent is to increase the involvement of all parents in the selection of secondary-level courses and programs of study, as well as in the formulation of postsecondary plans. Although the objective is to improve communication with parents of students in the academic middle, the program is for all parents. An emphasis is placed on "structure." It is recommended that a strategy to involve parents be highly structured: Parents should understand the purpose of the program—better academic and postsecondary planning for their children—and know when the critical decision points in high school program course selection are and how to use data provided by the school to evaluate their child's ICP.

The program begins with a meeting of eighth-grade parents.

Step 1: Have an Eighth-Grade Parent Meeting

The best time to involve parents in the tentative formulation of secondary and postsecondary plans for their children is when they are getting ready to start high school. This time is strategic and the best opportunity to get their attention and involvement. Most high schools have an orientation meeting for parents, but this is a one-shot effort, not concerned with anything other than orientation. Unless a student is exceptional in either a positive or negative sense, parents hear or receive nothing further from the high school except during report card periods. This point is particularly true of the parents of academically average youth; they are less apt to initiate meetings with teachers.

We recommend a parental involvement program that is considerably more extensive. This program would be explained during an eighth-grade meeting; other activities would include presenting the five points that should be considered before decisions are made about a 4-year college education (as outlined in Chapter 7). The major purpose of this meeting would be to acquaint parents with the school's expectations of them and to hear what they expect of the school. Specifically, school administrators would expect the parents to be active participants in the development of their child's tentative career plan and to be part of and an extension of the school's career guidance program. As such, parents should expect (a) to be called together periodically during the next 4 years and (b) to periodically be given objective data that enable them to test, with their children, the continued reality of the earlier developed career plan. In addition, parents would be expected to help expose their children to different types of jobs and postsecondary opportunities and to be understanding, patient, and willing to consider alternatives in which their child may express an interest.

Two points need to be stressed when providing parents with information about their child's academic progress in relation to the ICP. The first point is the issue of providing objective data. There is quite a difference between a guidance counselor (a) telling a parent that his or her daughter is not "college material" and pointing out that her cumulative average and SAT test score do not compare favorably with those of successful college students and (b) telling parents about educational alternatives that may meet the adolescent's goals more effectively. Announcing that a child is not college material can have a personal pejorative connotation. The second method relays the same information but does so more objectively. Parents—particularly parents of those in the academic middle, the anxious class—can be expected to hold high hopes that their children will obtain 4-year degrees. They will respond best to objective data and positive alternatives.

The second point is that clearly defining the roles for parents and schools will facilitate the delivery of objective data and thus make high school educators more willing to provide it and parents more open to accept it. The school's purpose is to provide parents with feedback regarding the appropriateness of their child's tentative career plan, the program of study they have chosen, and the courses they are selecting. The school will help parents evaluate these data if they wish. This critical message should be delivered to eighth-grade parents: "We want you to be involved in the formulation of your child's tentative career plan. We will at specific times provide you with data to test the continued reality of this plan. We will help you evaluate this information if you wish, but we are not here to make the decision for you. It is your choice." After all, because parents make the decision, they will have to live with it; but they have a right to expect the school to provide the guidance and data needed to make a sound one.

The basis for this strategy is a "compact" between parents and school. Prior to the 1970s, high school teachers and guidance counselors took a very directive role in student programs of study and course-taking decisions. In the late 1970s and the 1980s, the pendulum swung the other way: The shopping mall high school emerged, students and parents made all decisions, and the schools stopped providing specific course-planning direction. Youth thus received little to no satisfactory guidance. A compromise could resolve this situation. A compact between the school and the parents would require the provision of highly structured guidance through objective data and counseling; the presence of these elements would help parents and students make informed decisions.

Step 2: Involve Parents in the Career Plan

We argued earlier that creating *other ways to win* begins with more effective systematic career guidance. The focal point of this effort was an ICP for each student. This plan may best be formulated before a student enters high school, but some formal review process or development of this plan for each student should occur in the first semester of the freshman year, if it has not already occurred. This plan should represent a joint effort or decisions by each student and his or her parents. If nothing else, parents should approve the plan. This process may sound bureaucratic, but human nature being what it is, people tend to take something they sign a little more seriously. Any number of other things can be done to involve parents, such as sending them periodic reminders about their child's plan. Whatever efforts are expended, the objective is to get parents to take responsibility for systematic collaboration with their children in this planning and to get them to confront the facts.

Step 3: Provide Objective
Feedback at Strategic Times

Parents need to be involved not only in the development of their child's ICP but also in the periodic reality testing of this plan as their child's academic credentials evolve during 4 years of high school. National survey data (NCES, 1988) reveal that current first tentative career plans of 80% or more of students will include pursuit of a degree from a 4-year college or university. Other national data also show that, on average, only about 30% of high school students will graduate with credentials that suggest this path is a good idea. The objective of the third step in the parent involvement plan is to provide data that give parents and students the opportunity to test the reality of the 4-year degree plan and that permit them to alter plans, if necessary.

The types of feedback that can be provided to parents include test results; course grades in strategic courses, such as math, science, and foreign languages; and PSAT, SAT, and ACT test results. The key is to relate the data to the child's tentative career plan. A report card performs one function, but a report card with a note from a school staff member suggesting that a child's performance is inconsistent with his or her tentative career plan is a much better wake-up call. This type of feedback is most effective when delivered at key points in a student's high school career, particularly at the end of the sophomore and junior years. In some cases, key pieces of objective data, such as PSAT scores or SAT scores, arrive in the spring of the junior year—an excellent time for a review of ICPs.

Step 4: Provide Opportunities
for Individual Assistance

The final step in the plan to involve parents in the secondary and postsecondary planning process is simple: Provide parents with the option of individual advising from guidance staff or teachers. Every piece of correspondence and every meeting with parents should end with instructions for contacting the school for "individual attention." Of course, this proviso also means that counselors must be available at night and on Saturdays on a rotating basis because today the parent who does not work during the school day is the exception. It would be nice to think that the response will be so overwhelming that not enough staff will be on hand to handle the requests. Realistically, however, this probably will not happen. Nonetheless, the option should always be present, and as efforts to create *other ways to win* begin to pay off, responses will increase and guidance staff can begin to do more of what they were trained to do in the first place.

Five Points to Make With Parents

When working with parents, it is important to continuously stress the following five points.

Point 1. The School's Role Is to Help You Make
the Best Decision for Your Child, Not to Make the Decision for You

It is critical to continually stress with parents that your role is not to make decisions for them nor to tell them what their child should or should not be doing after high school. Many parents get very defensive, if not suspicious, when the schools begin suggesting that their hopes and dreams for their teen are not realistic. On the other hand, every parent hopes to make the best decision for his or her child. Parents are more receptive to the message, "The decisions are yours; our responsibility is to provide you with help and information to make the best decision." Many will choose to ignore both the information and the offers for help, choosing instead hope and prayer that all will work. Many, however, will respond positively to this message. As an aside, this message is important to stress with staff as well. Often educators interpret career development programs as ultimately telling teens what they should do. Not so! The goal is to help them make more informed decisions.

Point 2. Focus on Postsecondary Success,
Not on College Admissions

Parents who graduated from college during a time when admission was relatively competitive may consider the concern for ability to do college work over successful admission to college to be heresy. At first, they may not understand this message. They may assume, naively, that college acceptance implies the admitted can do college-level work. The reader should know better by now. Although getting into a college of choice may not be guaranteed, getting into "a college" is guaranteed. The real issue, then, is not admissions, but graduation. A related point to make is what predicts success in post-secondary education. Yes, academic skills are important, but having a career goal is as important. In fact, as argued previously in this chapter, it is now more important.

Point 3. Know the Odds and Know the Costs

Perhaps the message that parents and students need most to hear is also the most difficult to deliver; namely, among those who try baccalaureate education, losers outnumber winners. Only about one half graduate in less than 6 years. Among those who do, one third to one half end up in jobs they could have gotten without a college degree. Because no one wants to deliver the bad news, it is easier to look the other way. But students and parents deserve to know. Another point that should be kept in mind: Although some surprises are inevitable, odds are that the poorer a student's academic credentials, the greater the likelihood that he or she will end up a statistic in the losing column. Parents and students can no longer count on colleges to deliver the bad news through rejection letters. In these times of excess higher education capacity, one can be sure that colleges will be the last to deliver the message. The high schools have to handle this task.

Point 4. If the Goal Is a Better Job,
Then Do Not Confuse Education With Occupational Skills

When working with parents, particularly if the objective is to motivate the parents of students in the academic middle to consider *other ways to win*, it is important as well as effective to stress the earlier referenced five points before the decision is made to pursue a 4-year college degree. Thus, this message is important for all parents. The ranks of underemployed college graduates include many bright graduates who got baccalaureate degrees but not in a major whose skills equate with demand in the labor force. Remember this point: High earnings are a reward for skills in demand. The demand for workers with skills learned at the baccalaureate degree level is much too low to accommodate the 1.3 million who graduate each year. At best, one in three will be underemployed. The path to economic security requires individuals to obtain skills that are in demand and necessary for many technical high skill/high wage jobs. Many of these skills can be gained both in school-to-career programs and in 2-year postsecondary technical programs. Some parents may counter that a better job is not the most important reason for getting a degree. This is true for some; these individuals need not be concerned with gaining occupational skills. For the rest—national survey data suggest 87%—whose goal is a better job, gaining skills should be important. If such students are determined to go to college, they should ask themselves this question: What majors will result in skills that will keep me from joining the ranks of the underemployed?

Point 5. There Are Other Ways to Win —
Consider All the Postsecondary Alternatives

The final message is the *other ways to win* message. This includes 1- and 2-year postsecondary education at the prebaccalaureate level, employer/employee-provided training such as apprenticeships, the military, and taking a year off to develop focus and improve academic skills. For a complete discussion of these alternatives, see Gray (2000). Remembering that the cornerstone of postsecondary success is having a career goal; an appropriate way to introduce *other ways to win* is to use the labor market information provided in this book. The key or path to *other ways to win* is high skill/high wage nonprofessional or gold-collar employment. The wages are excellent and the opportunities tremendous. Most require postsecondary education but at the prebaccalaureate level. It is the best postsecondary education investment in America; 1 or 2 years cost less than 4, and often one's employer will pay the cost of continuing to get a 4-year degree.

Other Ways to Win

In this chapter, we have outlined the first steps that need to be taken to create *other ways to win* for those in the academic middle. We argued that the success of any such efforts would require informed decisions by teens and their parents—thus, the importance of career development/guidance programs. These programs have three major goals: (1) to assist students to develop related career interests by the 10th grade, (2) to verify these interests in the 11th and 12th grades, and (3) to use this information to develop postsecondary plans. Parents are an important part of this decision-making process by teens; thus, how to approach them and with what message were also discussed in the chapter. The most important point to make is that these decisions are theirs and their teenager's to make. Our role is help them make the best decision.

If the goal is postsecondary success and presently few succeed, logic suggests the need to reexamine the high school program of study, or at least, the one that teens from the academic middle take. That is the topic of Chapter 9.

9

Step 2
Redesigning the High School
Academic Curriculum

In the United States, the abrupt cut-off that comes after high school graduation leaves a great many adolescents floundering, vaguely hoping for the best.

E. Herr and S. Cramer (1996), p. 8

The next step in creating *other ways to win* for high school students from the academic middle is to reengineer the academic/college prep curriculum. Why? Because the program was originally designed for the academically blessed, but now at least two thirds of all high students take this curriculum. In most high schools, the so-called college prep program is in fact the academic program for all but a few. Yet this program of study was never designed to meet the needs of all that currently enroll. Lacking any evidence that students will lose interest in postsecondary education, educators have little choice: Redesign the program of study to meet the increased diversity of students that now participate. The tactic we recommend is to develop parallel alternatives within college prep and organize to provide postsecondary placement services to all students, not just those bound for 4-year colleges. These parallel programs would differ in the postsecondary alternatives they are designed to prepare students for. Differing instructional modalities for use within these emphases are outlined in Chapter 10.

SECTION I

The Current Status of the College Prep Program

Prior to the 1970s, the college prep curriculum in United States high schools was a highly structured sequence of courses offering limited course selection options. Since the 1970s, this structure has largely faded away. The reasons for this ebb are many and varied, including the development of a "supermarket" array of options and a matching philosophy toward high school course offerings. This trend has been accompanied by a corresponding liberalization (some say decline) of admission standards at all but roughly 250 competitive colleges and universities.

In the past, completion of a college prep program of study was required for a student to be recommended by his or her high school for college admission and necessitated 4 years of specific college prep English, 3 years of college prep math, 2 years of college prep laboratory science, and 2 years of the same foreign language. This requirement is no longer applicable. Now, the typical high school program selection book begins with, "The following courses are 'recommended,' " then offers an amazing array of courses. Some of these are advanced, some regular, some remedial, some politically correct, and some designed to attract more students to a particular academic department. Importantly, even within content areas such as English or math, little or no effort is made to articulate or ensure sequential skill development among the many course offerings:

> Our point is that reengineering the college prep program of study does not mean dismantling a highly structured program of study, but instead requires putting some structure into a highly unstructured activity.

Also, it should be noted that high school educators have already bifurcated or created different emphases within the college preparatory program of study. Virtually all high schools have an honors program for the academically blessed, with very specific, demanding, and competitive courses. Meanwhile, those who need structure the most—the academically average students—dabble here and there in a highly unstructured, undemanding, and noncompetitive environment.

These honors programs hold an important key to creating *other ways to win* for those in the academic middle. First, the honors programs that exist in most high schools may be found under the overall rubric of college prep. In higher education terminology, they are a special emphasis within the college prep program of study. Thus, the first step in creating alternative emphases within the college prep program has already been taken and paves the way for additional emphasis to be developed. Second, this honors emphasis is centered around a unique focus; everything about it is aimed at preparing those enrolled to be competitive in making the transition from high school to selective colleges and universities. Thus, the honors program is unique, not just because the academically blessed are there, but because the emphasis itself has a specific transition goal.

It is proposed that the precedent of developing a unique emphasis within the college prep program aimed at unique transitional goals, pioneered through the development of an honors curriculum, be continued by adding other emphases aimed at preparing other college prep students for different transitional goals.

A Proposal for the Redesign of the Academic Curriculum

Building on the example of the honors emphasis that currently exists within most high school college prep programs of study, we propose that the curriculum be reengineered to add other emphases for students who aspire to different types of higher education. A schematic design is provided in Figure 9.1.

The proposed design has three phases: (1) a common core of academic courses for all students in the 9th and 10th grades, (2) four different transitional emphases in the 10th and 11th grades, and (3) transitional postsecondary placement services in the 12th grade.

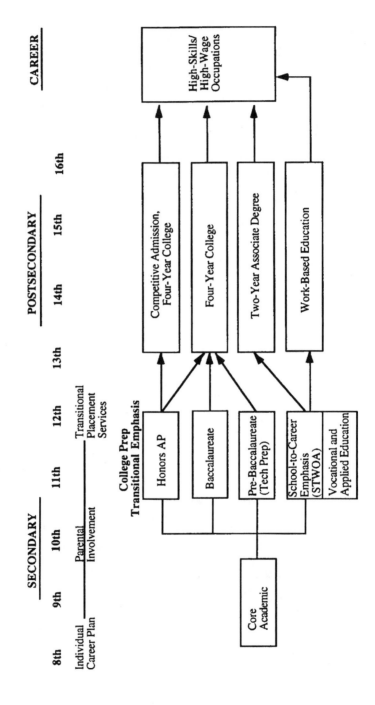

Figure 9.1 College Prep Redesign

136

Phase 1: Core Academics

The core academic component is best viewed as a common academic curriculum approach recommended by numerous educational reform reports. All ninth graders whose individual career plans (ICPs) include postsecondary education take a specific set of prescribed academics that includes English (with an emphasis on reading for comprehension and writing), traditional college-level math (algebra, geometry, or more advanced courses for those able to take them), science (including laboratory biology), and at least 1 year of foreign language (the second year being completed by 11th grade). This freshman and sophomore year experience not only forms the academic basis for the last 2 years of high school but, equally important, also provides objective academic performance data that students and parents can use to make decisions about the emphases to complete in the 10th and 11th grades.

Regardless of the postsecondary plans actually pursued, requiring this strong academic program in the 9th and 10th grades will prove beneficial. Strong basic academic, critical thinking, and problem-solving skills have been identified by the U.S. Department of Labor's SCANS report (U.S. Dept. of Labor, 1991) and numerous others as prerequisites for success in any type of high skill/high wage work.

Tentative Career Choices

The second goal of Phase 1 is to help students develop several related career interests by the time they must choose a transitional emphasis in Phase 2. In schools that have career pathways or career major programs, helping students reach this level of career maturity is the objective. Likewise, the individual career plan is designed to provide a structure that helps students make individual career interest decisions as a prerequisite for Phase 2. At the end of the 10th grade, students are asked to select one of four transitional options. This decision should be based on an evaluation of tentative career interests and academic record to date.

Phase 2: Transitional Emphasis

In the 11th grade, students must select one of four transitional emphases within the college prep curriculum. Two of the four already exist: One is honors/advanced placement (AP). Another exists by default—the largely unstructured, relatively undemanding college prep course taken by those who are not qualified for the honors/AP program. We call this second emphasis the "baccalaureate emphasis." Two other emphases should be added officially. The first is a prebaccalaureate or tech prep emphasis design that will prepare students academically and technically for success in 1- or 2-year postsecondary education programs that lead to high skill/high wage careers. The second is a school-to-career option that prepares teens for full-time employment after graduation. Within this emphasis there can be two options. The first is a work-based learning/cooperative education model; the second is a more traditional school-based technical/vocational education model. High schools that do not have a technical education facility would opt for the work-based model. Each of these emphases is described later. Importantly, whereas the honors and baccalaureate emphases are composed exclusively of academic courses, the other two emphases include technical skill instruction and work-based learning in the 11th and 12th grades.

Verify Career Choices

While teens are progressing through the program of study in their chosen transitional major, they will also need structured assistance to verify the tentative career choices. As discussed in Chapter 8, these activities can include job shadowing, internships, externships, paid employment, volunteer work, interviewing for information, guest lecturers, and so forth. Verification of career interests is critical during these years, as it is the number one piece of information used to develop postsecondary plans in Phase 3.

Phase 3: Transitional Placement Services

The final component of a redesigned college prep program of study is the provision of placement services to all students. Thus, services for those going to 2-year technical colleges, work-based learning programs, or regular employment will be identical to those already provided for students applying to competitive colleges. This placement effort should be viewed as the culminating activity within the systematic career guidance program recommended, as well as the implementation of the ICP recommended in Chapter 8. Although placement is now traditionally viewed as a guidance function, a look at the ratio of counselors to students reveals that this point of view is impractical. Thus, placement of the graduating class must be the responsibility of the entire staff. Everyone on the faculty knows something about a service or option that could assist in placement. Everyone must pitch in.

Summarizing, these three components are offered to reengineer the college prep program of study. This proposal is admittedly a departure from the current shopping mall philosophy. In fact, it is quite directive. In the first 2 years of high school, students are given little latitude. The only latitude will be in the different courses for students who enter the ninth grade with more advanced math, science, and foreign language skills and in social studies and other electives.

Student performance in the first 2 years, as well as their tentative career choices, will be used in conferences with parents about the selection of an emphasis for the last 2 years of high school. Each high school administration must decide how directive it wishes to be regarding the election and completion of an emphasis. Many may worry about parents' reactions to a more directive, prescriptive approach to high school course selection.

Parental Acceptance

After years of allowing students to select courses without regard for need, high school educators may be leery of parents' reactions to a more structured program of study. Recent studies suggest, however, that the public is actually looking for a such a program. In a poll reported in *Education Week* (Walsch, 1994), 84% of parents polled believed that high schools should be more prescriptive; many thought that students who had not mastered basic skills should not graduate.

Students agree; 43% in the Shell Poll indicated that they did not get adequate help selecting courses in high school. Change will not be easy: Parents are anxious about the future of their children, and the *one way to win* mentality is deep rooted. These are among the reasons that recommendations for creating *other ways to win* started with career guidance for students and help with higher education planning for parents. Yet, the costs of higher education and the increasing number of reports about underemployed college graduates are making everyone more receptive to a new message. Parents want more structure in the schooling of their children. A highly structured 9th- and 10th-grade academic program and 11th- and 12th-grade transitional emphasis, which are required in order to be recommended to a postsecondary institution, are a response to this concern.

Two New Transitional Emphases

We propose the addition of two new transitional emphases to the existing two (honors and baccalaureate) that officially or unofficially exist within the traditional academic program of study. The intent of both is to prepare students from the academic middle for transitions into settings in which they can learn skills that are prerequisites to competing for high skill/high wage jobs that do not require a baccalaureate degree. One is a postsecondary technical education emphasis (prebaccalaureate) designed to prepare students for success in 1- and 2-year technical postsecondary education programs. The second (school to career) is an emphasis designed for students seeking full-time employment after high school. This emphasis has two options: work-based learning and vocational technical education.

The Prebaccalaureate Emphasis (Tech Prep)

The prebaccalaureate emphasis is an old idea whose time has come. It is a variation or refinement of the 2-plus-2 concept: 2 years of high school education that lead to 2 additional years of postsecondary education. The emphasis goal is to motivate and prepare high school juniors and seniors to successfully pursue 1-and 2-year programs of postsecondary technical education. These programs are cooperative efforts of high schools and postsecondary technical education providers. A schematic of tech prep programs is presented in Table 9.1.

Typically, tech prep programs are organized around specific occupational clusters or majors. For example, a health occupations cluster or major would be designed to prepare students for a transition to a variety of postsecondary 1- and 2-year technical programs in the health field. The key element is the articulation agreement.

TABLE 9.1 Prebaccalaureate (Tech Prep) Emphasis

High School 11th & 12th Grades		Postsecondary Technical Education
Focused academics	Formal articulation agreements	1- and 2-year technical programs
Related technical education		

The Articulation Agreement

The most important element in the tech prep transition program is the articulation agreement that formally links high schools with postsecondary technical education providers. These agreements form the basis both for organizing the junior and senior year academic and technical education component and for identifying the "perks," or benefits, to be accrued by students who participate in the program. The agreements specify three things: (1) what academic and technical competencies students are expected to have mastered in high school in order to be admitted into and successful in the specified postsecondary program or programs, (2) how these competencies will be assessed by the postsecondary provider, and (3) what benefits will accrue to graduates who have these competencies.

For example, an articulation agreement related to an associate degree in architectural engineering would specify math and science competencies; adequate computer skills, including familiarity with computer-assisted drafting; and other academic requirements that form the academic focus of the junior and senior year academic and technical program of study. The agreement would then state how these competencies will be assessed. Often, this assessment is accomplished through course grades. A better approach, however, is some type of more formal assessment, such as portfolio or performance skill assessment, that leads to a clear message to students and parents regarding readiness to pursue this postsecondary option. Finally, the agreement specifies the benefits to be gained by students after participating in this transitional emphasis. That last item is the key to everything.

Motivating Students to Participate in Tech Prep

Although much has been written about the merits of tech prep programs, little has been said about students' reasons for taking them. Yet, high school educators know that this is the key issue. Why would students and parents choose this program over the baccalaureate emphasis within the college prep program? Improved systematic career guidance that includes an ICP, programs of postsecondary planning and counseling for parents, and objective data regarding each student's academic performance will go a long way toward motivating students, particularly those in the academic middle, to elect this option. Additional incentives will also help.

Incentives for students to participate in a prebaccalaureate emphasis take three basic forms: (1) advanced standing, (2) advanced standing with time shortened, and (3) preferred admissions. The first allows students to enter the postsecondary technical program with advanced standing; certain courses normally required are waived. These courses are often in the technical area—thus the importance of opportunities for vocational technical education course work in the junior and senior year academic program. This advanced standing leaves open the second incentive, shortened time, which means that the postsecondary program of study will take less time and fewer tuition dollars to complete. Postsecondary providers are not always willing to negotiate such time-shortened options. Students still benefit, however, from the opportunity to take more advanced courses or additional electives for the price of a standard certificate or degree.

Another powerful incentive emerges when admissions to relevant postsecondary programs are competitive. Programs in certain 2-year technical health occupations that typically turn students away are a good example. In these cases, students who complete the technical education emphasis and meet the expected competencies are given admission preference. A final incentive is an arrangement in which those who meet certain academic and technical education standards in their junior year and first semester of their senior year are allowed to begin their certificate or associate degree program as college students during their last semester in high school. Obviously, this option is not possible in many local high schools, but when possible, it is a very powerful motivator and is popular with parents.

Regardless of the incentive outlined in the articulation agreement, the essential point is to be able to demonstrate to parents and students clear advantages to participating in these prebaccalaureate or tech prep transition emphases. This is why so much importance is attached to a written, formal articulation agreement. Experience with tech prep transitional programs across the United States has shown that the credibility of such a program increases dramatically with both students and parents when it is viewed as jointly sponsored by the high school and one or more postsecondary institutions. In some cases, the specific incentive will be preferred admission; in others, it is the promise of a degree for less money or a better degree for the same amount of money. Of course, these emphases have one other benefit: some likelihood of academic success.

The Transitional Academic Program

Whereas the linchpin of tech prep programs is the articulation agreement, the heart of these programs is the focused academic course work that takes place in the junior and senior years. The content and skill levels for this curriculum are dictated by the articulation agreement. Recommendations for these courses are discussed in Chapter 10. It should be emphasized that most of this course work will not require the addition of many new courses, but rather the redesigning of courses that already exist. Remember that because these students are already in the college prep program of study, they will be taking math and science in their junior year and—as recommended in Chapter 10—should be taking math and science in their senior year as well. The obvious need here is for a refocusing of the courses already being offered. One possible exception is science courses. Typically, few high school students take physics or advanced biology, yet all students in these technical emphases will need one or the other. The problem is that these students do not need the same physics or biology courses that will be needed by students preparing for a 4-year engineering or biology degree. In cases like these, new courses will need to be developed.

The School-to-Career Emphasis

The school-to-career emphasis within the academic program is for those students whose postsecondary plan includes full-time employment. Follow-up data suggest that many of these students will also become part-time students as well. The core academic program

TABLE 9.2 School-to-Career Emphasis

Option 1: Work-Based Learning		
School-Based Learning	Connecting Activities	Work-Based Learning
Focused academics OJT Job readiness training Job shadowing	School/industry compacts	Formal

Option 2: Career and Technical Education		
Focused academics	School-based technical training	Capstone work-based learning

in the 9th and 10th grades should have given them the prerequisite level of academic skills to prepare for high skill/high wage employment that does not require postsecondary education.

There are two designs, or options, that can be used in the school-to-career transitional emphasis: work-based learning and school-based career and technical education. The objective of both options is to provide students with occupationally specific skills that lead to labor market advantage when they apply for jobs after high school.

Option 1. Work-Based Learning

In this option, the occupational specific skill instruction takes place on the job in the workplace: thus the term *work-based learning*. It is similar to the school-to-work and the youth apprenticeship programs of the 1990s. As illustrated in Table 9.2, students in this option receive focused academic courses in the first 2 years of high school just like everyone else. However, they also take a course or courses in job-readiness skills that stress safety, appropriate work habits, and ethics. Equally important, students participate in a series of job shadowing experiences to facilitate the choice of work-based learning at specific sites in the last 2 years of high school.

As a basis for the work-based learning, the school works with co-operating employers to assist them in the development of work-based learning sites and experience. Unlike cooperative education programs of the past, the school takes a more active role in developing and monitoring the work-based learning to ensure that students are exposed to a variety of job experiences and thus receive skills training.

During the junior and senior year, school-to-career students in this option become part-time paid employees as well as full-time students. The work-based instruction often takes place during the school day but provisions are made to continue academic instruction in communications and applied math and science.

There are two significant advantages to this option. First, for schools that do not have a modern career and technology program, or have a program that is over-enrolled, the work-based option provides a very realistic way to provide excellent job preparation. Second, for the students, the advantage is part-time employment that phases nicely into full-time employment their senior year. If they are at all successful, their work-based learning site becomes their full-time job when they graduate. Often their work experience during the high school years leads to an advancement in pay or credit in an apprenticeship program when they graduate. Often employers encourage a student to pursue postsecondary education part-time and they pay for it.

The school-to-career emphasis has two unique features: (1) During their final years in high school, students will begin to participate in a work-site learning program on the job; and (2) after they graduate, they continue that program as full-time employees. Participants may also attend 1- or 2-year postsecondary technical education institutions on a part-time basis, often at employer expense. Prior to the work-based learning in the 11th or 12th grades, most employers require that students have relevant introductory technical training, including relevant safety instruction. Both of these are typically provided via high school vocational education programs, as is discussed in the following. To accomplish this work-based learning, schools will have to develop various "connecting activities," such as the formulation of school/industry compacts to develop work-based learning sites or provision of assistance to on-the-job trainers in such areas as instructional techniques. Many high school staff are already certified in cooperative education; they can lead these efforts. In fact, this emphasis can be conceptualized as a type of cooperative education program (not to be confused with cooperative or group learning techniques) for a different student cohort.

There are numerous examples of effective school-to-career programs. The Pro-Tech Program in Boston is one such example. In the final 2 years of high school, students spend a good part of the school week in Boston health care facilities in work-based learning experiences. If they are successful in the program, they transition to full-time employment at these sites after graduation and continue their training as part of the facility's ongoing staff development effort. In addition, many attend community college part-time. The essential feature of this and similar programs is that, in the final 2 years of high school, students retain the status of full-time high school student, but much of their education takes place on the job. Thus, after they graduate, the transition to full-time employment is almost seamless.

Apprenticeships

Arguably the best school-to-career opportunity that can be arranged by a school is the transition to a registered apprenticeship program. Registered apprenticeships (endorsed and regulated by either the federal or state departments of labor) are run by both employers and workers' groups and, almost without exception, are in high skill/high wage occupations. An important and often misunderstood element in the success of such programs is that they require a relatively high level of academic ability, including reading for comprehension, computational skills, and problem solving by using science principles. This reality led a RAND study of the apprenticeship to conclude that the most promising prospects for these programs were students who "enter postsecondary education directly after high school but never obtain a degree" (Finegold, 1993, p. 5). This is exactly the group we have argued would benefit from the creation of *other ways to win.*

Unfortunately, the availability of registered apprenticeship programs varies dramatically across the United States. As a result, this option for school-to-career programs may not be available in all communities. Where they do exist, they are one of the best roads to high skill/high wage work.

Option 2. Career and Technical Education

This option is a revitalized version of traditional vocational education and is superior in teaching prerequisite job skills in high skill/high wage occupations that do require postsecondary education. Importantly, many students who participate in this curriculum become upwardly mobile and go on to prebaccalaureate technical education as a result. In this model, the instruction is still school based; the curriculum is totally under the supervision of educators. The option is best linked, however, with a work-based "capstone" learning experience in the senior year. A complete discussion of the role of this program of study follows later in the chapter.

Motivating Students to Participate in School-to-Career

Why would students even consider a school-to-career option? At first, it seems highly unlikely. Remember, however, that a percentage of academically average students, even when they take a college prep program, go to work rather than to college after graduation. They may do so after realistically considering their motivation, academic skills, and the costs involved in attending college. It is difficult to pinpoint exactly when these students make the decision not to go to college, but the Class of 1998 Follow-Up Study (Gray & Xiaoli, 1999) found that students from the academic middle who went to work instead of to college were already working 20 hours per week while in high school. Thus, it is highly likely that they will begin developing strong connections to the workplace about the same time they could legally work, which for most is also about the time they start their junior year. Viewed from this perspective, it seems very likely that during their junior year—certainly by the beginning of their senior year—some college prep students have already, no doubt quietly, opted for employment, not college. Although these students may be unwilling to enroll in a concentrated vocational education program and thus lose face, they would be interested in and certainly would benefit from a school-to-career option within college prep.

Also, it is important to remember that many employers who offer these formal training programs also provide tuition reimbursement for relevant postsecondary education courses that lead to a degree. Thus, a student can participate in a paid formal training program and go to college part-time at no net expense; this would be a strong incentive for some students and parents.

Finally, it is well to keep in mind that many students decide early, for a variety of reasons, to continue their education part-time while working full-time. Typically, however, they end up working in dead-end jobs for low wages. The school-to-career option offers a decidedly better opportunity for this group of students in that it allows them to go to school part-time but also to begin a high skill/high wage career, instead of earning minimum wage.

Postsecondary Placement
Services for All

The third component and final phase of a redesigned college prep program of study is a commitment and (re)organization of staff to provide transitional postsecondary placement services for all students, not just to those applying to competitive colleges. This assistance for all students clearly does not happen now. In fact, all too often, many of those in the academic middle never talk with a guidance counselor during their entire 4 years in high school. In all fairness, high school guidance counselors give help to all who ask. The problem is that, in most cases, neither those in the middle nor their parents ask for it. Thus, in too many cases, counselors with huge client loads take an I-am-here-if-you-need-me approach. The academically blessed—those who need help the least—show up for services; the unblessed do not. This dichotomy should no longer be acceptable. Creating *other ways to win* requires a commitment to provide structured postsecondary placement services for all students, regardless of program of study or postsecondary goals.

The transitional placement commitment begins with a caseload philosophy. This means that the faculty view the entire senior class as needing directive placement assistance and organize to provide these services. Schools can be organized in a variety of ways to do this, but in most cases guidance counselors cannot do it all. Another approach, then, is the placement team approach. The senior class is divided into groups, and teams of faculty/administrators/paraprofessionals—anyone else working in the building—are formed. Each team is assigned responsibility for a student group. In such an effort, a guidance counselor can be assigned to each group to provide postsecondary planning expertise. The placement team's job is to provide significant individual attention and individual help in making a successful transition from school to postsecondary education or career.

A comprehensive postsecondary placement effort by high schools that aggressively seeks out all students and offers help is very important in the creation of *other ways to win* for those in the academic middle. Many of these students do not get as much direction from home or have the range of role models available as do their more academically blessed peers; thus, they flounder. Instituting a systematic career guidance program that centers around ICPs for all students will help, but a large dose of individual attention for each student by a member of the high school faculty, particularly during the senior year, would do a world of good to ensure that those in the invisible middle make a successful transition from high school.

SECTION II

The New Role of High School Career and Technical Education

The focus of creating *other ways to win* has been on reengineering the academic program of study. The rationale for this focus is that this program includes many of the academically average youth. Unless something catastrophic happens, it is unlikely that this trend will be reversed. What does this mean for vocational education—now called career and technical education—and what about those students who go to work instead of college? Although as important as ever, like academic education, vocational education will need to be reengineered to accommodate a new role—preparation for 1- and 2-year technical education—while maintaining its traditional role, preparation for full-time employment.

The continued importance and future role of high school vocational and applied education is perhaps best illustrated by its prominent role in the School to Work Opportunity Act (SWOA, 1994) of the

1990s. Although the title of this act suggests that its purpose is to facilitate the transition from high school to work, closer examination of its provisions suggests it could have been called the School to Career Opportunity Act because it requires programs to have educational components that include both secondary and postsecondary technical education. The important point is that the drafters of the bill recognized the importance of vocational technical education at the high school level as a prerequisite for success in 1- and 2-year postsecondary technical education.

Furthermore, a transitional emphasis within the academic curriculum that has a technical education component has one other important advantage: It provides some fallback skills for those who go to work instead of to higher education. A rather consistent 20% of high school graduates enter the labor force each year. In times past, a majority of those who went to work would have participated in vocational education programs such as business education, vocational agriculture, or trade and industrial education. Having concentrated in vocational education and been aided in job placement assistance by vocational education teachers, these students made an orderly transition from school to work. Most had jobs before they graduated, and most jobs offered full-time employment with benefits.

Today, many of the students who in the past would have taken career and technical education now dabble in the college prep program but do not go on to higher education; instead, they seek regular employment. As revealed by the Class of 1998 Follow-Up Study (Gray & Xiaoli, 1999), most of these students got minimum-wage jobs in retailing and food service; they were not prepared to compete for entry-level high skill/high wage work because they had no skills. If they had taken a transitional emphasis within the college prep program of study that included some technical education, they would have had basic occupational skills to be competitive for some types of high skill/high wage employment when they decided not to continue their education. Thus, the two additional transitional emphases—prebaccalaureate and school-to-career—that should be added to the college prep program of study must include some technical education.

Vocational education, therefore, does have an important place in the high school curriculum. However, the mission of vocational education will, in the proposed model, be expanded from concentration in course work that will prepare students for full-time employment at graduation (this will continue to be important for some students) to a curriculum that offers shorter (semester) courses for college prep students who choose a transitional emphasis design to prepare them for postsecondary prebaccalaureate technical education or work-site school-to-career options.

Also, as noted, that some students will still need traditional vocational education. The large and growing percentage of students with special needs who take a concentration in vocational education proves the continuing need for a program of study designed to prepare students for full-time employment on graduation.

For most students, however, vocational education offerings will provide the background technical skills needed to increase the probability of success in postsecondary technical education and even baccalaureate-level education. A case in point involves high school business education courses. Some students will continue to take the 3-year business education sequence of skills courses in preparation for entry into the workforce after graduation. Even greater numbers will take business education courses, because they provide essential skills such as keyboarding and word processing for all those who are college bound, and accounting and spreadsheet courses that are important for those with aspirations toward employment in business or engineering. Another example is high school vocational education drafting programs: Some students will take this vocational sequence in preparation for full-time employment as drafters (because many are still hired directly from high school). Most in this curriculum, however, will actually be preparing themselves for certain types of postsecondary education, such as engineering and architecture, wherein computer-assisted drafting skills will have to be mastered. A final example is high school health occupations: Some students will take the full course sequence in preparation for full-time employment as paraprofessionals in the health field. Other students with aspirations toward a postsecondary education in the health fields will take health occupations single-semester courses designed to prepare them for prebaccalaureate or baccalaureate education.

In essence, then, the creation of *other ways to win* does not diminish, but in fact increases, the value of a strong high school vocational technical education component. Such a program does three important things. First, it provides a relevant program of study for those who are work bound. Second, it provides an important source of technical skill training that is a prerequisite to successful 2-year technical education programs and that provides a fallback for those in the academic middle who take the baccalaureate option but go directly to work after graduation. Third, many vocational technical programs provide important opportunities to learn specialized skills needed by the 2- and 4-year college bound. Thus, a viable vocational education integrated into the comprehensive high school curriculum is a necessary element in creating *other ways to win*. In high schools that do not have access to vocational education, other appropriate alternatives can often be developed within technology education and home economics and in the community.

Other Ways to Win

In this chapter, we have argued that because most high school students take a college prep/academic curriculum, creating *other ways to win* requires that this curriculum be redesigned to be more effective for the diverse student cohort now enrolled in it. Building on the reality that this program of study has already been bifurcated into honors and nonhonors, we recommended that two additional emphases be added. One (prebaccalaureate/tech prep) prepares students for 2-year technical education; the other (school-to-career) prepares them for work-based formal training and part-time postsecondary education. The goal of these emphases is to effectively educate those enrolled so that they will be academically successful in whatever postsecondary pursuit they choose. In many cases, new courses will not be needed, but it is clear that teaching and scheduling them in the same old way will not work. Furthermore, the educational modalities by which academically average youth learn best are often different from those most effective with the learning styles of the academically blessed. This situation is discussed in Chapter 10. We also argue in Chapter 10 that if these students are to become more involved in the new options, high school faculty and administrators must stop treating them as second-class students.

10

Step 3
Ensuring Equal Status
and Focused Academics

The Strength of the Wolf Lies in the Pack.
Rudyard Kipling, *The Law of the Jungle* (1865-1936)

Those in the academic middle often feel about high school the way second- and third-string athletes feel about filling out the roster, serving as the competition in practice, or riding the bench: Technically, they are part of the team and must dutifully show up for practice, but their real involvement is minimal and subservient. Their major role is to be spectators in uniform. They get little or no attention from the coaches and often are treated as unwelcome baggage.

This same role is played by the majority of high school students who make up the academic middle. They are enrolled, come to school, and attend class most of the time, but they are there in body only. Their real engagement in the curriculum is nil. They are passive to the point of being almost invisible. Some people would argue that this "invisibility" is their fault, but considering the amount of attention they receive from high school staff (typically none), who can be surprised at their passiveness? The way they act mirrors the way they are treated. When they do manage to get someone's attention in school, the treatment they get differs considerably from that given to their more gifted peers. The academically blessed are treated by teachers as future peers; the less blessed are treated as future subordinates and, in many ways, inferior. This culture must change if high schools are to become more effective for those from the academic middle.

Often, relatively little effort is made in the high school classroom to reach those students who populate the academic middle. Just having to teach these students is considered by some to be "hardship duty"; status among high school teachers comes from teaching honors and AP courses. Even though a majority of those in the academic middle now take so-called college prep courses, these courses are still taught in the same modalities as when only the academically blessed took them. The attitude seems to be, "OK, if you want to take these courses, we cannot stop you; but if you don't learn, it's your fault, not mine." Likewise, few teachers make much of an effort to motivate these students whom they now find taking their college prep classes. Both of these situations must change if high schools are to become more effective for those from the academic middle.

In the previous chapter, we outlined a plan that would redesign the college prep curriculum to better meet the postsecondary transitional needs of those who now enroll. In this chapter, we discuss three other fundamental aspects of this reform: (1) the need to change the culture of high schools to increase academic expectations for students who make up the academic middle, as well as the amount of time, energy, and personal attention they receive from the faculty, a process we call "ending Taylorism"; (2) the need to modify the overall educational modalities by which these students are taught in order to increase learning; and (3) the need to make renewed efforts to motivate and challenge this generally uninvolved cohort.

SECTION I

Putting an End to Taylorism

It is very unlikely that academically average students will be more engaged in the high school curriculum unless they feel more a part, a more valued part, of school itself. To use an analogy, although multitudes may dutifully show up at church on Sunday, only those who feel like a real part of things show up at the potluck suppers and other church functions; those who feel like an unwelcome or unimportant part of the congregation will generally stay uninvolved. Those in the academic middle share this feeling. Thus, if the goal is to transform these youth from spectators of the academic process to active participants, they will need to feel important. At present, they are treated as unimportant and inferior. If educators want to make them distinctive, they must be treated as distinctive.

As part of the Class of 1998 Follow-Up Study (Gray et al., 1998), the researchers sought to determine the degree of alienation of those in the academic middle. Scant actual evidence of alienation was found, but when these youth were asked whether "some students were treated better by the faculty than others," 84% said yes. Interestingly enough, this double standard was not missed by the more academically blessed either; 75% of the most academically successful students also observed that some students were treated better than others.

Most readers can simply recall their own high school experience to verify the dual standards or differing treatment of students, depending on their status among staff. Some students, the academically blessed, and certain athletes could roam the halls at will, unquestioned, whereas the mere sight of others in the hall was enough for a teacher to call the office. Nothing has changed; high school still has a double standard. This dual standard is not necessarily the result of a widespread pejorative attitude toward those in the middle, although undoubtedly some of this exists among some staff. Instead, it stems from an ideology held by teachers about children and the role of the school. It is most reminiscent of a set of beliefs called Taylorism (with a little bit of social Darwinism thrown in).

Defining Taylorism

Although students may be taught in school that the United States is founded on the principle that all are created equal, they learn in school, particularly in high school, that apparently some of their peers are more equal than others. In every high school in the United States there is a predictable "in crowd"—those anointed and honored by teachers, school administrators, school boards, and school policies. Predictably, they are mostly the academically blessed, although some with special athletic prowess or well-connected parents may join the ranks. The point is that most high school educators take this situation as perfectly natural and even desirable because of 90-plus years of Taylorist influence on the schools.

Although Frederick Taylor (1856-1915), the father of scientific management, was a proponent of close cooperation between workers and managers, his theories of organizing for efficiency were interpreted differently. In brief, managers were to assume "all burden of gathering the traditional knowledge which in the past had been possessed by the workmen" (Taylor, 1911, p. 83). Thus, in the Taylorist model, the importance of managers increased dramatically and suggested that only those of high intellect were capable of assuming this role. Meanwhile, the level of intellect needed by the worker diminished significantly; in fact, the Taylorist model suggested that the fewer decisions the workers had to make, the better. The important thing was that they learn to do as they were told. The bottom line, from the Taylorist frame of reference, was that the academically blessed were destined to be the captains of industry and thus infinitely more important to the nation than the less academically blessed, who were destined to be subordinates.

Taylorist Influences on High Schools

The division of labor implied by scientific management quickly became a fundamental paradigm that structured the expectations that educators had for the increasingly diverse student population at the turn of the century, especially for students in high school. As argued by economists Samuel Bowles and Herbert Ginitis, the success of capitalism came to be viewed as dependent on a "minimal participation in decision-making by the majority of workers and protecting (the power, prerogatives, and privilege of) a single minority of managers" (quoted in Cole, 1988, p. 2). The role of the school as a social institution came to be viewed as teacher of this social order. This is not to say that high school teachers, most of whom were first-generation college graduates, set out deliberately to train those in the middle to be drones. Still, that is exactly what they did, seduced by the belief that they were justifiably rewarding merit. The typical attitude among high school educators and the public was that the privileged status that some students enjoyed was simply a reward for their hard work; the conventional wisdom was that these students were the most meritorious because they worked the hardest. Thus, any special privileges or attention they may have received in return were deserved. This same rationale buttresses current discriminatory policies, such as weighted grading.

Challenging the Taylorist Rationale

The rationale of merit that justifies Taylorist practices in high schools has many flaws. One is that most of the more academically successful students succeed, not because they work harder, but because they were born academically blessed. Powell et al. (1985), for example, found that in private high schools where performance pressure was evenly applied, the brightest students reported working the least. Parents of the most successful high school students often seem a bit bewildered about their children's performance because the youngsters do not seem to work very hard at their studies; typically, they do not—they are simply academically talented. The hardest-working students in any high school are probably the average students who, through hard work, overachieve and graduate with respectable academic credentials. Thus, policies that discriminate against the academically average teen are misguided.

A second flaw is the attitude that somehow the academically blessed are more important to the prosperity of the United States. Modern economic realities suggest that the opposite may be true. Lester Thurow (1992) of the Massachusetts Institute of Technology (MIT), for example, suggests that the real problem is not the education of the academically blessed, but rather the education of the rest. In nation after nation, it has become clear that it is not possible to compete successfully in a global economy with only an educated elite. Workers at all levels must be equipped to change with change and to have the literacy and numeracy skills required of emerging occupations. Perhaps the key point in the "total quality management" philosophy of Deming is the equal importance of all workers and the need for collaboration; the Taylorist view of the manager as a source of all information and the savior of the common worker is old-fashioned. The new economic order requires all workers to be a part of the team, but it is difficult to figure how the workforce of the future is to learn this value and these interpersonal skills when the first major organization they belong to—namely, their school—is run in the opposite fashion.

The basic irony of this treatment of students in the academic middle is that, as Thurow suggests, these students may be more important to the nation's economy than most college graduates. For example, it is largely the students in the academic middle, the non-college graduates, who find themselves as the backbone of the technical, skilled, clerical, retailing, distribution, and transportation systems of the nation. As any administrator knows, it is the clerical support staff of the organization, most of whom are high school or 1-year business school graduates, whose skills, insights, and loyalty literally make the organization function. So it is with the vast array of individuals who hold jobs in craft, precision manufacturing, and customized repair occupations that make the economy function. These vital elements of the national and, indeed, international infrastructure rely on a constant infusion and availability of youth from the academic middle, most of whom enter the labor force with a high school diploma or a prebaccalaureate technical degree/certificate, not a 4-year college degree. Given their importance in an era of shortages of skilled workers, their effective education and their being treated as a precious national asset should be a national, state, and local priority. (Herr, 1995).

For those who seek to create *other ways to win* for those in the academic middle, ending Taylorism is not only an egalitarian issue but also an educational imperative, because it is closely linked to self-esteem, curriculum engagement, and the overall motivation of these students. When graduating high school seniors are asked to describe themselves, the academically blessed exhibit considerably higher self-concepts than those in the academic middle. More disturbing, the academically blessed not only have good things to say about themselves but often have pejorative things to say about the less blessed. In fact, there seems to be a dual problem: Students in the academic middle generally have a rather low opinion of themselves, whereas the academically blessed graduate with serious delusions of grandeur. It seems that Taylorist assumptions do not serve either group very well.

Strategies for Ending Taylorism

It will be difficult to motivate those in the academic middle unless Taylorist attitudes and practices are eliminated in the schools, particularly high schools. Such efforts may also infuse some much-needed humility into the academically blessed. The following strategies are recommended.

Challenge the Culture: The Equity Audit

Taylorist attitudes have been around for five generations. They will not go away unless challenged in the same way people question attitudes about race, gender, and the environment. One does not change attitudes, however, by putting educators on the defensive. Change theory would suggest that a better approach is to let them discover they may unconsciously have been doing the wrong thing. One way to reach this discovery is through a faculty-led "equity audit." The intent of this internal audit is to simply document time, services, and preferential policies that have different effects on different groups of students. For example, divide the senior class into three academic groups by using the criteria suggested in Chapter 4. Then calculate such things as average class size and document the services provided by guidance, participation in special trips and seminars, and so on. The results will be obvious: 30% of the students will be getting 50% to 70% of the institutional resources and attention. The question then is this: Is it OK to be doing this? And if not, what should be done about it?

Challenge Discriminatory Policies and Practices

Just about every high school in the United States contains policies and practices that discriminate in favor of the academically blessed at the expense of those in the academic middle. Although the word *discriminate* may seem strong, the U.S. Department of Education's Office of Civil Rights does not regard it as too harsh. It has made segregation of students within schools a target of its enforcement efforts ("Amherst School," 1994). The Lawyers Committee for

Civil Rights Under Law has worked to make ability grouping a central issue in the Wilmington, Delaware, segregation case, and similar action led the San Jose, California, school district to drop its ability grouping system ("Amherst School," 1994). In Amherst, Massachusetts, in response to a challenge from parents of average youth, most of whom were minorities, a review panel recommended to the school board that the district drop the "use of weighted grades, class ranks, and courses labeled 'basic,' 'standard,' and 'advanced' " ("Amherst School," 1994, p.1).

Is it too early to say that these cases are an early signal of changing attitudes toward policies and practices that favor the academically blessed? It may be, but it also is a sign that high schools functioning in this way are vulnerable in the courts. Although some of these practices, such as AP and honors courses, may be justified, giving extra weight to grades in these courses is not; John Dewey would call it "cruel and illiberal." Policies and practices such as these send the wrong messages to all children: To the blessed, it leads to illusions of grandeur; to the less blessed, the message is they are second rate. In these times of litigation, it may be only a matter to time before weighted grading goes the same way as single-gender gym classes. In reality, the practice is somewhat comical because it leads to mathematical impossibilities: In high schools with weighted grading systems, it is not uncommon for a student to graduate with a GPA of greater than 4.0 (A); this fact explains why most competitive colleges first evaluate a student's high school records by recalculating or unweighting his or her GPA so that it can be realistically compared with those of others who apply. The point is that schools committed to creating *other ways to win* for those in the academic middle should debate these policies. These debates should include a representative group of parents and the public, not just the advocates of the academically blessed.

Stop the Obsessive Rank-Ordering of Students Against Each Other

Even at the worst of high schools, it can be predicted that the senior class will be ranked from top to bottom in terms of academic performance. High schools seem obsessed with rank-ordering students. The grading system of most teachers is designed first and foremost to rank-order the class. If you do not think so, imagine what would happen if a teacher gave all students an A; even if they all mastered the material, the teacher would be risking serious condemnation by peers and administrators as being too easy.

When one is challenging the obsession with rank-ordering students, it is effective to point out the implied philosophy behind this practice, namely, that for some to look good, the rest must look bad. The logical extension is that for some to look really good, a lot have to look bad. When teachers announce that they rank on a curve (and most do, whether they admit it or not), they need to understand what is implied: The objective of the evaluation is to rank-order the class, not to evaluate learning. To understand this issue better, let's consider the case of the President's Physical Fitness Award and the attitude of teachers toward this evaluation. Interestingly, although teachers and parents would consider it outrageous if everyone received an A in English, they would think it was great if everyone achieved sufficient physical fitness standards to receive the President's Award. What is the difference? First, the award is based on a set of very objective criteria, such as the ability to jump so far, run so fast, and so forth. Second, because it is an objective standard, the competition is against the standard, not against other students, and therefore there is no need to rank-order students against one another. The goal is to make all learning fit this paradigm, whereby the goal is to achieve the standard, not to do better than other students in the class. This is a far cry from current practice. The point is that if for some to win big, the rest—namely, those in the academic middle—must lose, why should they try?

Seek a Way to Integrate Students of Differing Academic Ability

Most high schools begin the day with something called homeroom period. Homeroom is truly a unique phenomenon because it is probably the only circumstance, other than lining up alphabetically for graduation, in which the school does something that results in bringing high school students together on an egalitarian basis, independent of course selection, intellectual ability, athletic prowess, family income, or even race. More needs to be done to promote this intermingling among students of differing academic characteristics. Particularly detrimental is the segregation of students according to program of study; such division amounts to segregating students by ability. Although perhaps not by design, the realities of scheduling classes are that the academically blessed often end up in the same classes. Likewise, those in the academic middle spend their high school careers interacting with others in the academic middle. Arguably, this practice does not serve either group well, but it is particularly harmful to those in the academic middle and perhaps explains why these students go unchallenged, unmotivated, and unengaged and why some teachers hate to teach them.

A commitment to those in the academic middle calls for doing things to end their isolation. Finding ways to ensure interaction among students of all academic abilities should become an obsession. One tactic is the institution of a portfolio requirement in which the portfolio team must include a mix of students from varying curricula to jointly plan and complete selected learning tasks or projects. Another is to resist ability grouping and to do whatever is possible to correct what occurs naturally because of the master schedule. For example, one alternative is not to put all students enrolled in calculus in the same social science class.

Create a "One Team" Culture

The final strategy is perhaps the most important. Although most high school mission statements suggest an interest in all students, they are, in fact, elitists; that is the culture. This condition needs to be changed. Kipling reminds us that the strength of the wolf lies in the pack; schools should embrace this philosophy as well. The desperate need is to convey this message to students on a daily basis: All are equally valued, no one is better than anyone else, arrogance is frowned upon, humility is valued, and harassment will not be tolerated. The goal is to go from having an *in-group* to having *one group*. This conversion will not happen unless the principal, teachers, and guidance counselors are committed to creating such an environment.

SECTION II

Modifying Instructional Modalities and Practices

In the first section of this chapter, we argued that creating *other ways to win* for those in the academic middle begins with changing the treatment of these students. Only when these adolescents feel equal, not inferior, can educators expect them to exert equal efforts. The next step is to ensure that instructional modalities and practices used in college prep courses populated with academically average students match their learning styles.

Matching Instruction and Learning Styles

The following six strategies are offered as ways to improve the instructional effectiveness of the high school college prep program of study to make it more effective for the growing diversity of students who now enroll.

Emphasize Contextual, or Applied, Learning

The dominant instructional modality in most high school college prep classes is the "student/copying machine" model of instructional effectiveness. Teachers lecture, students copy down in their notebooks what the teachers say, and on tests students are asked to reproduce their notes. Although cognitive learning researchers suggest that this is the least effective instructional modality for all students, the academically blessed, perhaps because they are blessed, master the student/copying machine game early in their high school careers and become quite good at it. When the content itself becomes more and more abstract or detached from the real world, their performance, in comparison with that of students in the academic middle, becomes even better because those in the academic middle learn best when the instructional modality and the material itself are "applied" (see Bottoms et al., 1992).

The dilemma for those in the academic middle who now enroll in college prep courses is that they are taught primarily in modalities not appropriate for their learning styles. For example, national studies of high school classroom instruction find that only 18% of teachers spend more than 10% of class time putting the course content into a real-world context (U.S. Department of Education, 1994). High schools committed to creating *other ways to win* for average youth need to address this instructional modality mismatch.

Contextual or applied learning strategies may be worth considering for all students. Research by the Southern Education Board revealed a fascinating inconsistency: Although vocational education students' scores on the NAEP test were lower than the scores of students in the college prep curriculum, the gap was significantly closer in problem solving than in math knowledge. Thus, vocational education students did much better on the problem-solving items than would have been predicted on the basis of their performance in math courses. This finding leads to speculation (Bottoms et al., 1992) that, when math is taught in a real-world context, as occurs in vocational education, students learn to apply the knowledge and are better problem solvers, a worthy goal for all students, even those heading off to Ivy League colleges. John Dewey (1900) wrote that "education through vocation . . . combines within itself more of the factors conducive to learning than any other method" (pp. 82-83).

In applied learning modalities, the content is grounded in the real world; the learner is active, not passive; and the emphasis is on problem solving, knowledge, and skills that are needed by problem solvers. Although the student/copying machine instructional modality is measured in terms of what students know, the contextual modality is more interested in what students can do. One such example is the City Watch program at Ridge Tech in Cambridge, Massachusetts, where the entire ninth-grade curriculum is taught within the context of an exploration of the students' community. Mathematics, for example, is taught by using the local community as the content to be numerated, measured, and otherwise described in mathematical terms.

Such dramatically different approaches are not necessary, however. What is necessary is a commitment by teachers to face the fact that their earlier instructional methods may not be effective for the growing number of academically average youth who now take college prep classes. Unfortunately, more than a few teachers take the "blame the learner" approach; that is, if students do not learn from a teacher's instructional method, the trouble must reside in them, and not in the teacher. After all, the better students seem to be doing just fine. This point of view may be one good reason for the fact that the fastest-growing groups of courses in higher education are remedial. Facing the challenge of academically preparing those in the middle to be successful in 2-year technical education requires a change to contextual learning modalities.

Emphasize Reading for Comprehension

When one looks closely at enrollments in remedial courses in higher education—those that are required but do not count toward a degree—we see that an interesting trend has developed. The percentage of students who must take math has actually gone down a bit, but the percentage of students who must take remedial reading has gone up. Remember that almost one fifth of semicompetitive students in the Class of 1998 Follow-Up Study (Gray et al., 1998) reported being required to take remedial English; in other words, they were found to be deficient in reading for comprehension. The point is that if educators assume that the majority of those in the academic middle will continue on to higher education, preferably in 2-year technical programs, the goal is to ensure that they do not have to take remedial courses. This point translates into an important reality: High schools need to face the fact that many students graduate with poor reading skills.

Over the years, the college prep English classes have changed little. In some cases, the literature selections have been modernized, and more emphasis has been placed on writing. In times past, English teachers who taught college prep courses could be assured that their students were good readers. Today, this assumption is false. Contemporary adolescents as a group do not spend as much time reading for pleasure as those of the past; they watch television instead. Those who seek to create *other ways to win*, which include ensuring the success of students who select these alternatives, must face the fact that the instructional objectives of high school English now must include improving student ability to read.

Emphasize Math and Science for All Seniors

For the average youth graduating from the academic middle and heading off to college, remedial English and remedial math seem to be almost certainties these days. We have just addressed the reading issue; now, what can be done about math and science? This question is complicated by the finding in the Class of 1991 Follow-Up Study that many academically average students who ended up in remedial math and science courses had taken above-average levels of math. In many cases, those who had to take remedial math courses had taken 3 years of college math in high school. The trouble was that very few had taken a math course during their senior year. Thus, these students entered college not having taken any math for nearly a year and a half. No wonder they end up in remedial courses. The same pattern was found for science. Those students who most need to take math and science in their senior year, those in the academic middle who head off to higher education, are the least likely to be found in these courses in the 12th grade.

In light of these findings, it is recommended that every effort be made to encourage all students to take math during their senior year in high school. For those whose tentative career choice is a post-secondary program that will require science—all paraprofessional health careers—taking science in the 12th grade is likewise important. One way to accomplish this goal is to adopt local graduation policies that require 4 years of math and science to graduate, a practice that has been in place in the Connecticut Regional Vocational High School system for years.

Teach Keyboarding and Computer Software Skills

One cannot be successful in higher education without gaining the ability to use a standard keyboard effectively and to use standard software packages, especially word-processing, spreadsheet, and telecommunications software that now provide access to everything from the card catalog of the campus library to the worldwide Internet. Likewise, computer skills are as important today to those who aspire to high skill/high wage work as physical strength was to the craftsperson of the past. In the modern workplace, computer skills have replaced manual dexterity and strength. Preparing students from the academic middle to be successful in pursuing prebaccalaureate education that leads to technical high-wage work, therefore, requires adequate preparation in both keyboarding and software manipulation.

Evidence from the Class of 1998 Follow-Up Study (Gray et al., 1998) suggests that most high school graduates, regardless of their academic credentials, may be graduating with inadequate computer skills. Even among those graduating with academically competitive credentials, only 48% indicated entering college with adequate computer skills. As might be expected, even fewer (38%) of those in the academic middle reported having adequate computer skills. Importantly, among this group, very few had taken a computer-intensive course in high school, and more than half had not taken a beginning typing course that would provide them with keyboarding fundamentals. Yet, remember that more than half of those graduating with academically noncompetitive credentials now enter college, where computer skills are a necessity; those who lack such skills are at an immediate disadvantage.

Experiment With Portfolios and Cooperative Learning

A *portfolio* is defined here as a collection of evidence or products that demonstrates a student's ability, as opposed to his or her knowledge. This emphasis on application is important for all students but is particularly successful with academically average students. Although some states, most notably Vermont, have experimented with portfolios as a replacement for more traditional high school assessment techniques, such dramatic departures from present practice probably will not occur. Instead, it is recommended that a portfolio requirement be added to current graduation requirements. Doing so sends a message to all students—even to teachers who need to get the message—that, in schools, both knowledge and ability are valued. This message has the potential to be a strong motivator of academically average youth.

Portfolios have another potential benefit: to increase the interaction of students and thus end isolation based on students' course selections. Portfolio policies can be developed to encourage collaborative or cooperative efforts that reach across program lines. The key words are *collaborative/cooperative efforts* and *peer learning*, new words for students' collaborative work in "groups."

Consider Block or Intensive Master Scheduling

A block or intensive master schedule typically replaces the standard 7-period high school day with a 4-period day plus lunch. Instead of being the typical 55 minutes, each period is now 90 minutes. The result is that courses normally taught over 180 days can be completed in one semester. Thus, a student interested in math could take eight math courses in high school. Unlike the typical high school schedule in which students take five or six courses each semester, in this plan students typically take only three major courses. This latter point is the reason for our recommendation of block scheduling.

Whereas the academically blessed can take five or six major courses each year, less able students often cannot handle so many different courses and different demands. They do much better when they are able to concentrate on three. This has been the experience at Hatboro Horsham High School in Pennsylvania, which uses block scheduling. Teachers reported that, whereas the achievement of the best students remained high, the achievement of those in the academic middle increased significantly. Block or intensive scheduling has many other advantages as well, including significantly greater flexibility for creativity in the development of additional emphases within the college prep program of study (as recommended in Chapter 9). The major advantage, however, is that average youth are allowed to concentrate their efforts on fewer subjects during a semester.

SECTION III

Motivating the Academic Middle

When asked to describe those in the academic middle, high school teachers typically have some difficulty—in itself, a testimony to the invisibility of these students. The most-cited characteristic is their lack of motivation. Probed further, teachers view these students as generally taking the easiest route in order to do as little as possible. Although some are very interested in certain aspects of the high school experience, in general, they are not very interested in their course work. The accuracy of this perception is not debated here. In fact, research conducted as part of the background for this book confirmed that, compared with their more academically blessed and successful peers, this group of students is largely not engaged in the curriculum; when it comes to academics, many may as well be taking correspondence courses. The issue, then, is not whether they are unmotivated, but how to motivate them.

Strategies for Motivating
the Majority

There is little doubt that the majority of those in the academic middle can be motivated. In fact, most are motivated to do many things with great enthusiasm and energy; the problem is that the list does not include schoolwork. How does one motivate these youth, then? Some suggested strategies follow.

Develop Career Motives for Learning

Unlike the academically blessed, who perform even the most irrelevant academic schoolwork out of a sense of duty or foreknowledge of their future success, those in the academic middle are not so motivated. Academic work is often difficult for them, and they have received little reward for their efforts; thus, they will not make an extra effort unless they believe it can make a difference. The most important connection to help them make is that it will make a difference when they graduate. Thus, we recommend that teachers of college prep courses populated by those in the academic middle make concrete efforts to relate classroom activity to probable future course work in higher education, which currently is the career goal of most in this group. This strategy has the potential for greater success if a good job has been done in developing the students' ICPs (see Chapter 8). Vocational educators have found, for example, that even the most recalcitrant and limited students can be motivated to learn basic academic skills when they see the need for them in the type of work they plan to pursue.

Have High Expectations
for All Students

Throughout this book, the limited expectations of teachers for those in the academic middle have been both documented and discussed. In our view, these limited expectations ultimately limit motivation. Human nature is such that, lacking intrinsic motivation of the type developed in the first strategy mentioned previously (develop career motives for learning), most will do only what is demanded. The motivational force of such demands should not be overlooked.

At present, little is asked of students from the academic middle even when they take college prep courses. In fact, it is not uncommon for students to drop vocational education courses because they demand more work than college prep courses taken by average students. The most direct result is that when these students graduate, they end up in remedial courses that are very expensive and that predict fairly accurately that a student will not graduate from college. A more productive strategy both for students and parents is to demand more from these students: to ask them to seek personal excellence in what they do, rather than simply getting by. Most students will respond to this external motivation. Not everyone will, of course. High expectations will mean that students who in the past got Cs—given as gifts by teachers to keep the peace when they should have got Ds or even Fs—will now receive the grades they deserve. This experience will cause some degree of discontent among some parents, but not only is it the ethical thing to do, it is also in the best interests of those whom it will make the most unhappy. Better a D or F in high school that leads to plans other than pursuing a 4-year college degree than $40,000 in financial aid debt and no degree, which occurs in all too many cases.

Improve Academic Self-Concepts
by Catching Students Doing Things Right

This strategy is borrowed from the book *The One Minute Manager* (Blanchard & Johnson, 1982). Those in the academic middle need more old-fashioned attention and recognition from their teachers. A key to academic motivation is a positive self-concept about one's ability. Those in the academic middle typically have a low academic self-concept and are in the college prep program because they can see no other way to win. Little wonder that these students have negative academic concepts. During their first 8 years of school, teachers gave them negative feedback by catching them doing something wrong. Contrast this with the feedback received by the more academically blessed. They have had 8 years of teachers catching them doing things right.

A useful example of catching people doing things right is the one used by Blanchard in the film *The One Minute Manager*, in which he asks the viewer to remember how parents act when they are trying to teach children to walk. In short, they watch for even the smallest sign of success and then praise the children. Contrast this approach with another alternative, namely, punishing a child for attempts that are anything less than perfect steps. This sort of treatment would cause most of us to still be crawling around. Yet, the latter approach may all too often be that applied to academically average youth throughout high school. In particular, teachers should begin by positively reinforcing effort and then work on achievement by catching students making small improvements and praising these efforts.

Other Ways to Win

In this chapter, we began by arguing that if the goal is to ensure postsecondary success for all high school graduates, then high schools must (a) stop treating all but a few students as second-class citizens and (b) take a hard look at the instructional modalities and practices within the college prep curriculum now taken by most students. Specific strategies were offered to achieve both. These steps, plus the implementation of a systematic career guidance plan that includes an ICP for each student and a redesign of the college prep curriculum to include additional emphases aimed at alternative postsecondary alternatives, were recommended as ways to create *other ways to win* for graduating high school students, particularly those from the academic middle. All of these efforts are necessary because, as discussed in Part II of this book, the number of students who pursue a 4-year college degree in the hope that it will lead to a job in the professional ranks but end up not realizing this goal and the costs to individuals and the nation from this mass failure is staggering. Yet, despite the costs, one is left with a nagging question: Will such changes ever take place, and will the plight of academically average youth in U.S. high schools ever become part of the mainstream of the American educational reform debate? That question is the topic of Chapter 11.

11

Bringing "Average" Students
to Excellence

The term community *should be defined not only as a region to be served
but also as a climate to be created.*

The Forgotten Half (1988, p. 53)[1]

Creating alternatives for graduating high school seniors
should be a constant educational concern. Currently,
this is not the case. Events at a meeting of a local school's
strategic planning committee observed by one of the authors exem-
plify this situation. The purpose of the meeting was to develop questions for a follow-up benchmarking survey of recent high school
graduates, much like the Class of 1998 Follow-Up Study (Gray &
Xiaoli, 1999) referred to in this book. The leader of the group opened
the meeting by asking a rather straightforward question: "What did
members of the group want to know about their graduates that could
be asked on a questionnaire?" Everyone took a posture of involved
thought: Some looked at the ceiling thoughtfully; others rummaged
through the handouts for the meeting. Clearly, no one wanted to
speak up first. All were waiting for or deferring to those with power
in the group to set the tone and direction of the meeting. They did not
have to wait long. The superintendent of schools cleared his throat
and gave the group his most wisdomly posture; clearly, he was ready

to deliver a question of immense significance. Everyone waited expectantly. "I wonder," said the superintendent, who then paused briefly to build the suspense, "what happens to our kids who take calculus in high school?"

From then on, the rest of the meeting was predictable. Attention focused solely on the academically blessed. One member asked a question that pertained to students who went to work after graduation. Although everyone noted that this question was a concern, it clearly was not too great a concern, as the topic was quickly dropped. No one ever raised a concern about those in the middle group. This group had no advocates at this meeting, nor do they most anywhere else.

This scenario is played out in various ways day after day in U.S. schools. According to the National Center for Education Statistics (OERI, 1991), only 6% of all graduates take calculus in high school. Only about 40% complete a rigorous academic program of high-level math, science, and language courses. Yet, this minority receives a disproportionate share of the resources, most of the attention, and virtually all the recognition from high schools.

The purpose of this book is to bring to center stage the plight of those in the academic middle. Instead of asking about the academically blessed, we investigated the situations of the others. Research suggests that for every student who graduates with high academic credentials, two do not. Thus, it has been argued that the relevant question is not what happens to the one in three who heads to a prestigious college of his or her choice; data suggest that he or she is doing just fine. The relevant question is this: What happens to the other two in that ratio? In this case, data suggest that all is not well.

One of our particular concerns is those in the academic middle of U.S. high schools—those called by Powell et al. (1985) the "unspecial" because they are neither special needs students protected by legislation and taught in small classes by specially trained staff nor the academically gifted who are rewarded with the best teachers in equally small classes. Data suggest that, by and large, those in the academic middle of U.S. high schools are seriously adrift. They face a very uncertain future and get little help in preparing for it. The only message provided to them and their parents by the schools and seemingly everyone else is that there is only *one way to win*: trying to get a 4-year college degree in the hope that it will lead to a job in the professional ranks.

Challenging the *One Way to Win* Paradigm

Thus, the first message of this book is that the *one way to win* myth—the belief that future economic security can only be gained from a 4-year degree that will lead to a job in the professions—is, like all myths, mostly fiction with a dash of truth. Since the early 1980s, this widely held myth has been accepted almost without question by nearly everyone. Data from national surveys of graduating high school seniors demonstrate the wide acceptance of the myth. In such surveys, 94.7% report that they are planning to continue their education, 83.9% at the 4-year baccalaureate level. When asked to name the occupation they expect to be in at age 30, 49.3% of males and 68.8% of females cite "professional." Virtually all high school youth have the same career plan, the path recommended by the *one way to win* myth.

The *one way to win* message pressed on youth regardless of academic ability or interests comes from all sectors of society, but most notably from parents and teachers. According to an NCES study, 82.9% of high school sophomores reported that their mothers were recommending college, compared with 64.8% just 10 years before. Although parents may not be objective when it comes to their children's future, one might expect high school teachers and guidance counselors to be more so, particularly in advising academically marginal students to pursue interests other than a baccalaureate degree program. But data suggest the opposite. Between 1982 and 1992, the percentage of high school sophomores who said their teachers and counselors were recommending college doubled from 32.3% to more than 65%.

No doubt, both parents and high school faculty have students' best interests in mind. Their advice is based on a belief that today there is only *one way to win*. Unfortunately, they are misled and are giving well-intended but nonetheless poor advice to those in the academic middle. Although their intent is to ensure that adolescents will be winners in life, the advice they give often ensures the opposite for those in the academic middle. Instead, it ensures that they become a part of the college dropout or underemployment statistics.

The first hint that the *one way to win* advice may not be suitable for all is that among those who pursue a 4-year college degree, at best only half ever graduate. A close look at the academic credentials of high school graduates reveals the reason. The implicit assumption of those who indiscriminately provide *one way to win* advice to today's youth—that everyone is academically qualified to do college-level academic work—is not true. Viewed from a national perspective, only about 40% of those graduating from U.S. high schools have the credentials that predict readiness to do legitimate college-level work (see Figure 4.1). Thus, when a national average of 60% to 70% go directly on to higher education, it is clear that many who are admitted simply are unprepared.

Most of those who begin a 4-year college program academically unprepared spend their freshman year in college taking remedial courses. Although most colleges do not willingly publicize the percentage of incoming freshmen taking remedial courses, available data suggest that it is not uncommon today to find 50% of freshmen at some 4-year degree-granting institutions having to take one or more remedial courses. Although colleges do their best to put a positive spin on these courses, the fact is that they are the first predictor that the majority who take them will not graduate. Most ultimately cool out or fade away. The result is predictable: Nationally, of those who start a 4-year degree program, at best only half have graduated not 4, not 5, but 6 years later. And which are most likely to drop out— the academically blessed or the academic middle? Although admittedly too many of the academically blessed drop out, particularly in their freshman year, the likelihood is that most graduate in 4 years. Those from the middle, however, are the most likely never to graduate and probably should have considered other postsecondary alternatives, such as a 1- or 2-year technical program or a school-to-career option.

The second flaw in the *one way to win* advice is the scarcity of college-level jobs for those who do graduate. In the 1960s, only one in five 4-year college graduates failed to find college-level work. In the 1990s, it was one in three; in the professions, such as accounting or teaching, it was one in two. Again, the important point to ponder is this: Who is at greatest risk of not finding college-level work even after graduating? Is it the academically blessed who graduate from the most prestigious colleges with the best-connected alumni, or those from the academic middle who squeak through in 5 or 6 years and graduate from second-tier colleges? In the 1980s, big-name corporations, for example, recruited at more than 40 campuses; now they recruit at only a few prestigious and competitive colleges and universities. The likelihood that those from the academic middle will ever graduate from any of these institutions is next to none. Thus, those in the academic middle are the most at risk of being frustrated in realizing professional jobs in major corporations, even if they graduate from college. Such findings lead to the conclusion that the *one way to win* paradigm, though good advice for the academically blessed, is largely a myth for those from the academic middle. For those in this group who follow such advice, losers—those who drop out or end up underemployed and frustrated—will outnumber winners.

The third fault with the *one way to win* myth is its cost, which, in both unmet expectations and monetary terms, is huge. The number of underemployed college graduates who hold jobs they could have gotten after high school or who are returning to a 2-year technical postsecondary program to acquire occupational skills to get a decent job increases each year. Unfortunately, many of these young adults who cannot find college-level work have student loan debts to pay off. The dilemma is this: Fewer families can afford this cost of education. The growth in the student loan debt is evidence of families' growing inability to pay. This situation, accompanied by a national debt of approximately $4 trillion, leads us to wonder how much longer the United States will be able to provide such loans to so many persons without stricter criteria about recipients' abilities to do college-level work.

Finally, there is the unmeasured human cost to youth who early in life sense that the only valued thing to do after high school graduation—pursue a 4-year college degree—is clearly beyond their ability or what they can imagine as possible and thus give up. The need is for alternatives, for *other ways to win*, that can be effectively communicated to them and valued as ways to develop all our human resources.

There Are *Other Ways to Win*

The second message of this book is that there are alternatives, *other ways to win*, other routes to financial security and rewarding careers that should be particularly relevant to those in the academic middle, those most at risk of losing if they pursue the *one way to win* myth. This argument is developed in detail in Chapter 7. Suffice it to say that if the goal is an economically and personally rewarding career, the goal should not be education per se, but rather gaining the prerequisite skills necessary to compete for high skill/high wage work. The advice that such work can only be obtained with a baccalaureate degree is not true. Many high skill/high wage occupations in technical fields do not require a baccalaureate degree. Just as high skill/high wage professional work requires prerequisite skills, so too do these occupations require specific occupational skills. Unlike professional work, however, for which prerequisite skills are certified by baccalaureate or graduate school degrees, the skills required to obtain technician-level employment can be learned in either 1-and 2-year postsecondary technical programs or in school-to-career programs that include formal work-based preparation.

How well do these jobs pay? According to U.S. Department of Labor data, they pay very well. For example, individuals who successfully pursue high skill/high wage occupations, particularly in the occupational group identified as craft, precision metal, and specialized repair, as well as certain technical occupations in health and engineering, will earn more than all college graduates except for those baccalaureate degree holders who successfully pursue careers in the managerial or professional ranks. Meanwhile, unlike the more glamorous managerial and professional occupations, the demand for skilled workers in these fields greatly exceeds the supply.

Thus, there is *another way to win*, namely, obtaining the prerequisite skills for competing for high skill/high wage work that does not require a BA degree. The challenge is to reform the schools to motivate those in the academic middle to pursue these alternative ways to win. Redesign the high school curriculum to increase their propensity for success, and do it so well that parents will want their children to be involved. But will such efforts work?

Will Efforts to Create Alternatives Succeed?

Although veteran high school educators, especially those who teach college prep courses to academically average students, will readily admit a need for alternatives, their encounters with parents, school boards, elected officials, and so forth may well leave them skeptical about the viability of efforts to change the situation. As one counselor interviewed for this book put it, "Whenever I mention 2-year education to parents, I see their eyes glaze over. They have their minds set on a 4-year college." This counselor expresses a reality that cannot be denied.

The present mind-set in favor of 4-year college education will negate efforts to create alternatives for those in the academic middle of U.S. high schools. Yet, at the same time, it has been documented that providing only the 4-year alternative ensures that more than half who try it will fail and that the cost of this failure is terribly high. Thus, although the obstacles may be formidable, the need to create *other ways to win* is great. A design for creating these alternatives is presented in Chapters 8, 9, and 10. The recommendations are designed to meet the need to create an openness to alternatives, as well as an academic program to ensure that those who choose these alternatives are successful.

Reaching Out to Parents

The third message of this book is that parents are arguably the most critical variable in determining success of efforts to create alternatives for those in the academic middle. Survey research found that 82.9% of high school sophomores mention at least their mother as the individual recommending college. The unavoidable conclusion is that involving parents of academically average youth in secondary course selection and postsecondary planning is critical. These parents must be provided objective data about probabilities of their child's success in different postsecondary alternatives and the financial costs involved. In Chapter 8, a number of strategies are suggested for involving parents. Parents must be involved in the ICP process, especially the points at the end of the 9th, 10th, and 11th grades when a student's plans can be matched with his or her academic record.

At first, the majority of parents can be expected to resist anything but a 4-year college degree for their children. Aside from genuine concern about the economic future of their children, many parents are sometimes under intense social pressure to have their children attend a 4-year college. Yet, conditions are changing. Very few individuals can afford to send their children to college without borrowing money or taking out a second mortgage. Meanwhile, they are well aware from personal or friends' experience that many who graduate from college do not find the expected high-paying job waiting for them. The net result is that more parents are willing to consider alternatives, particularly if their child is not a great student.

Career Development/Guidance
for All Students

The fourth message focuses on the fact that the successful creation of *other ways to win* for those from the academic middle requires a systematic program of career development/guidance. This plan requires the involvement of both students and parents in its formulation and in structured "thoughtful confrontation" of career aspirations and academic achievement. Although the evidence for the need to create *other ways to win* for high school students from the academic middle is overwhelming, this in no way ensures the success of efforts. It is quite possible that much effort will be invested in redesigning the college prep program of study to include new emphases for those in the academic middle, only to have no one elect to take them.

Career development and guidance are equally critical in helping students and parents make postsecondary plans. Whereas most teens indicate that they plan to go college in order to "get a good-paying job," a career choice should be the foundation for making postsecondary plans. Most important, the focus or commitment that comes from having a career motive for pursuing higher education is now the most powerful factor predicting whether a student will graduate and find commensurate employment.

Career development/guidance programs should have three goals. First, by the 10th grade, the student should have identified one or more related career interests as the basis for course selection in grades 11 and 12. In the junior and senior years of high school, students should have the opportunity to verify these tentative choices as a basis for making postsecondary plans. Finally, all students should graduate with a postsecondary plan that has a high probability of success so that their hopes and dreams will be realized when they do.

Although career guidance is important for all students, it is important to understand the role it plays in ensuring the success of efforts to create *other ways to win*. The target group of students in our discussion, those from the academic middle, are the most likely to exhibit the signs of career immaturity. They do not know what to do, so they take what they see as the only alternative and passively prepare to go to 4-year colleges. They will continue to select this option unless an effort is made to develop a process in which they are forced to confront the realities of their plans and are provided with alternatives. They may still choose to pursue the *one way to win* myth. In fact, at first, most of them will; but over time, their involvement in a systematic career guidance program structured to provide them with data about the reality of their plans will lead them more and more to choose the two new options recommended to be included within a broad college preparatory curriculum.

Redesigning the
Academic Prep Program

The fifth message of this book is that creating *other ways to win* calls for doing things differently in U.S. high schools, particularly in the so-called college prep curriculum now elected by more and more academically average youth. Faced with the political reality that they cannot bar these youth from taking college prep courses and that failing most of them is also not an option, high school educators will have two choices. First, they can pretend that these teens are, in fact, preparing for college and let them slide through unchallenged and unprepared. Second, they can reform the college prep program of study to make it more instructionally effective for average students. Ethically, there is no choice. Doing nothing means continuing the downward spiral of these youth, leading to their enrollment in remedial courses at 4-year colleges and later dropping out after having collected significant levels of student loan debt. It is time to redesign the college prep program of study.

Specific recommendations to reform college prep are offered in Chapters 9 and 10. The redesign proposal centers around adding different emphases within the academic/college prep program of study and moving away from the shopping mall approach to a significantly more structured, sequential, and articulated curriculum.

In Chapter 9, we argued that virtually every high school in the United States has already bifurcated its college prep curriculum into two emphases—the highly structured and demanding honors/ advanced placement emphasis and a mostly unstructured, undemanding, unarticulated potpourri of college prep courses. We recommended two additional emphases. One prepares students to make the transition to, and to be successful in, 1- or 2-year postsecondary technical education programs that lead to high skill/high wage work. We call this the "prebaccalaureate technical postsecondary emphasis." The other is a school-to-career option. The goal of this emphasis is to prepare students to make the transition to, and to be successful in, one of a variety of employer-sponsored employer/worker group training programs in high skill/high wage occupations that now require academic skills commensurate with those taught in the college prep academic program.

It is important to assert here that these recommendations to add different emphases within the academic/college preparatory curriculum are not intended to make the education of the academically average student less rigorous or inferior. The intent is to make it different in the junior and senior years in order to prepare students to successfully pursue different postsecondary alternatives.

The redesign proposal calls for a departure from the take-what-you-want philosophy of student course selection that has predominated since the 1970s. We advocate the structuring of these emphases, meaning that students will follow a well-planned sequence of articulated courses—and the completion of one of the emphases by each student expecting the high school to recommend him or her to higher education institutions. The message to students and parents is this: Complete one of the four emphases if you expect the school to recommend you for any form of higher education.

This message may sound like too strong an assertion, especially to those who started their educational careers in the 1970s, during the advent of the shopping mall high school. Many may think that parents would not support a directive approach. National survey data suggest the opposite. The authors of a study conducted by the Public Agenda Foundation (Walsch, 1994) concluded that educators may be out of sync with parents on a variety of issues, including the degree of structure in the curriculum. Those in the sample were asked whether they believed that setting up clear guidelines on what students should learn and what teachers should teach in every major subject so that students and teacher know what is expected would improve academic achievement. Both the general public and parents overwhelmingly agreed, including 92% of parents of African American students. The public wants structure! We believe that parents of high school students would welcome clearly defined programs of academic courses that lead directly to alternative types of post-secondary education or other options.

In Chapter 10, we suggested strategies designed to make instruction within these four emphases more effective for academically average youth. Many of these strategies, such as emphasizing reading for understanding and mastery of computer software skills (e.g., word processing), are applicable to all. Other proposals, such as ensuring that all students take math and science in their senior year, are clearly aimed at those in the academic middle, who are the least likely to be found in these classes during their last year in high school. Their absence often results in the need to enroll in remedial courses in college.

One significant obstacle to effective educational redesign for those in the academic middle is the fact that they have been largely written off by some veteran high school teachers as unmotivated and lazy. Thus, in Chapter 10 we present strategies to motivate those from the academic middle. Although a number of approaches to motivating these students exist, they all begin with changing the treatment of these students in high school. Currently, those in the academic middle are largely relegated to second- or spectator-class status. Thus, why should anyone be surprised by their lack of motivation? Efforts to create *other ways to win* will work only if this aspect of the high school culture can be changed.

Challenging the High School Culture

The sixth message of this book is that the creation of alternatives for average youth will not occur without a groundswell of concern about this group from teachers, administrators, and school boards and without a willingness to try to change Taylorist attitudes. Creating *other ways to win* in U.S. high schools will require much work and the courage to stimulate much more thoughtful confrontation by parents and students regarding the reality of postsecondary plans. None of this will happen or will be effective without a change in attitude among high school educators about the relative importance of average youth. The policies and cultures of most high schools favor the intellectually blessed. Taylorism is alive and well in U.S. high schools; as long as it prevails, average youth will remain invisible and unmotivated.

Clearly, in the distribution of school resources, those in the middle do not receive their fair share. As reported earlier, even the courts are taking note of discriminatory practices such as weighted grading systems, disproportionate class sizes, and disproportionate allocation of resources and guidance services. These inequities have been tolerated for years because of the Taylorist attitude that the academically blessed are more important to society and therefore deserve special treatment. This is an old, unfair idea that needs to be challenged. It represents a form of intellectual bigotry that should not be tolerated.

Another aspect of challenging the culture is taking an honest look at the college prep program of study and recognizing its deficiencies. It needs to be redesigned. We see promising signs that high school educators sense this need. The rather quick spread of tech prep efforts across the United States can be interpreted as evidence that high school administrators, counselors, and teachers are well aware that the academic complexion of those who now take the college prep curriculum has changed and that something needs to be done.

One final element of the high school culture that needs to be challenged is the widespread belief in the *one way to win* myth by a majority of teachers and counselors. Data reported earlier indicate that the number of high school students who say their teachers and counselors advised them to go to college has doubled in the last 10 years. Considering the absence of evidence that the numbers of students who are academically prepared to do college work have doubled, we must assume that most teachers and counselors have bought the *one way to win* myth. They also have been convinced that getting a 4-year degree is the only hope for attaining success in society and therefore appear to be advising all but a very few students to give it a try.

We hope this book provides the reader with an understanding of the myth of *one way to win*. Educators who advise students on postsecondary plans have an obligation to know what they are talking about. According to the facts, there are *other ways to win* in which the propensity for success both in postsecondary education and future economic security is a lot higher for those in the academic middle. Those who seek to create *other ways to win* must challenge the prejudice that school staff have in favor of the 4-year baccalaureate degree. Educators must understand that, for the majority of youth in their schools, pursuit of a 4-year degree is a very risky proposition.

Doing What's Right

This book was written to draw attention to students in the academic middle of U.S. high schools. We sought to expose the false complacency that emanates from the belief that because most youth now enroll in the college prep program of study and go to 4-year colleges in record numbers, all is well. On the contrary, data reveal that, for the majority, all is not well: Of those who go to college unprepared, most fail either literally or fail to meet their aspirations to obtain professional jobs, and they often suffer great financial and personal costs in the process. But even if no costs were involved, educators have a professional obligation to treat all students equally. Clearly, those in the academic middle are not receiving their fair share of high school educational resources. Those from the academic middle have a right to equal attention, resources, and—when deserved—recognition. Their successes and failures are just as important to the larger society, to the community, and to their families as those of the academically blessed, and they should be just as important to their high school as well.

This chapter began with an account of a school district planning meeting. The dialogue at this meeting began with questions, not about the majority, but about how the few who took calculus were doing in college. This little scenario illustrates the preoccupation of public schools with the academically blessed and is played out in differing ways day after day, week after week, in U.S. high schools. It would have been significant if someone had said, "I think our real concern should be the students who did not take calculus." These students should take the center stage in the educational debate. These students need advocates. Maybe you will be one. Maybe the next time attention turns to the academically blessed, you will voice some interest and/or concern about the rest. After all, it is the right thing to do. It is the right thing to do for the adolescents involved and for attaining the appropriate balance of human resource development for the 21st century.

Note

1. W. T. Grant Foundation: Commission on Work, Family, and Citzenship. (1988, January). *The forgotten half: Non-college youth in America.* Washington, DC: Author.

References

American Council on Education. (1999). *The American freshman national norms for fall 1998.* Washington, DC: Author.

Amherst School urged to drop ability grouping (1994, October 8). *Education Week,* p. 1.

Anderson, E. (1990). *Street wise: Race, class, and change in urban communities.* Chicago: University of Chicago Press.

Anderson, L. (1983, December). Policy implications of research on school time. *The School Administrator,* pp. 25-28.

Barton, P. (1994, April). *Indicators of the school-to-work transition.* Princeton, NJ: Educational Testing Service, Policy Information Center.

Blanchard, K., & Johnson, S. (1982). *The one minute manager.* New York: Morrow.

Bottoms, G., Pressons, A., & Johnson, M. (1992). *Making high school work.* Atlanta, GA: SREB.

Carnevale, A., Gainer, L., & Meltzer, A. (1990). *Workplace basics.* San Francisco: Jossey-Bass.

Carnevale, A., Gainer, L., & Villet, J. (1990). *Training in America.* San Francisco: Jossey-Bass.

Chew, C. (1993). *Tech-prep and counseling: A resource guide.* Madison: University of Wisconsin, Center on Education and Work.

Clark, B. (1962). The "cooling out" function in higher education. *The American Journal of Sociology, 65,* 576-596.

Cole, M. (1988). *Bowles and Ginitis revisited.* New York: Faler Press.

College Entrance Board. (1993). *Annual survey of colleges*. Princeton, NJ: Author.

Dewey, J. (1900, April). Psychology of occupation [Monograph No. 3]. *Elementary School Record*.

Drucker, P. (1994, November). The age of social transformation. *Atlantic Monthly*, pp. 53-78.

Eck, A. (1993, October 4). Job-related education and training: Their impact on earnings. *Monthly Labor Review, 116*, 21-38.

Elfin, M. (1993, October 4). Does college still pay? *U.S. News and World Report*, pp. 96-98.

Finegold, D. (1993, March). *Making apprenticeships work* (RAND Issues Paper). Santa Monica, CA: Institute on Education and Training at RAND.

Fussell, P. (1983). *Class: A guide through the American status system*. New York: Simon & Schuster.

Gelatt, H. B. (1989). Positive uncertainty: A new decision-making framework for counseling. *Journal of Counseling Psychology, 36*(2), 252-256.

General Accounting Office. (1991). *Characteristics of defaulted borrowers in the Stafford student loan program* (Publication No. HRD-91-82BR). Washington, DC: Author.

Gray, K. (1980). *Support for industrial education by the national association of manufacturers: 1895-1917*. Unpublished doctoral dissertation, Virginia Polytechnic Institute, Blacksburg.

Gray, K. (1993, January). Why we will loose: Taylorism in the America's high schools. *Phi Delta Kappan, 72*(5), 370-374.

Gray, K. (2000). *Getting real: Helping teens find their future*. Thousand Oaks, CA: Corwin.

Gray, K., & Wang, D. (1989). An analysis of the firm size variable in youth employment using the NLS-Y data base. *Journal of Vocational Education Research, 14*(4), 35-49.

Gray, K., Wang, D., & Malizia, S. (1993). *The class of 1991: One year later*. Unpublished research report.

Gray, K., & Xiaoli, S. (1999). *A benchmarking study of the Class of 1998*. Unpublished research manuscript, Pennsylvania State University, University Park..

Herr, E. (1995). *Counseling employment bound youth*. Greensboro: University of North Carolina at Greensboro, CAPS publication.

Herr, E., & Cramer, S. (1992). *Career guidance and counseling through the life span* (4th ed.). New York: HarperCollins.

Herr, E., & Cramer, S. (1996). *Career guidance through the life span* (5th ed.). New York: HarperCollins.

Hilton, M. (1991). Shared training: Learning from Germany. *(U.S. Department of Labor) Monthly Labor Review, 114*(3), 33-37.

Holland, J. L. (1985). *Making vocational choices: A theory of vocational personalities and work environments* (2nd ed.). Englewood Cliffs, NJ: Prentice Hall.

Hossler, D., & Stage, F. (1992). Family and high school experience influences on the postsecondary educational plans of ninth-grade students. *American Educational Research Journal, 29*(2), 425-451.

Hoyt, K. (1994). A proposal for making transition from schooling to employment an important component of educational reform. In *High school to employment transition: Contemporary issues.* Ann Arbor, MI: Prakken Press.

International survey of faculty attitudes. (1994, June 22). *Chronicle of Higher Education,* pp. A35-38.

Jepsen, D. (1989). Adolescent career decision processes as coping responses for the social environment. In R. Hanson (Ed.), *Career development: Preparing for the 21st century.* Knoxville, TN: University of Tennessee.

Judy, R., & DiAmico, C. (1997). *Workforce 2020: Work and workers in the 21st century.* Indianapolis, IN: Hudson Institute.

McCormick, A., & Knepper, P. (1996). *A descriptive summary of bachelor's degree recipients one year later* (NCES Publication No. 96-158). Washington, DC: U.S. Department of Education.

Merriam-Webster's collegiate dictionary (10th ed.). (1993). Springfield, MA: Merriam-Webster.

Mohammed, A. (1998). *Participation in vocational education and underemployment among U.S. high school graduates.* Unpublished doctoral dissertation, Pennsylvania State University, University Park.

National Center for Education Statistics (NCES).(1988). *National educational longitudinal study of 1988* (NCES Publication No. 92-084). Washington, DC.: U.S. Department of Education.

National Center for Education Statistics. (1992). *Digest of educational statistics* (NCES Publication No. 93-299). Washington, DC: U.S. Department of Education.

National Center for Education Statistics. (1994). *Condition of education 1993* (NCES Publication No. 93-290). Washington, DC: U.S. Department of Education.

National Center for Education Statistics. (1997). *Condition of Education: 1997* (NCES Publication No. 97-388). Washington, DC: U.S. Department of Education.

National Center for Education Statistics. (1998). *Condition of education 1998* (NCES Publication No. 98-013). Washington, DC: U.S. Department of Education.

Naylor, R., Jr. (1994, September 1). Education gap widens to form anxious class. *Patriot News*, p. A4.

Oakes, J. (1985). *Keeping track: How schools structure inequality.* New Haven, CT: Yale University Press.

Office of Education Research and Development (OERD). (1991). *National longitudinal Study of 1988 second follow-up.* Washington, DC: U.S. Department of Education.

Passmore, D., Wall, J., & Harvey, M. (1996). *Community cost of technical skills deficits: A Pennsylvania case study.* Occasional paper, University Park: Pennsylvania State University, Workforce Education and Development Program.

Pennsylvania Economy League. (1996). *Building a world-class technical workforce.* Philadelphia: Author.

Powell, A., Farrar, E., & Cohen, D. (1985). *The shopping mall high school* (National Association of Secondary School Principals and the Commission on Educational Issues of the National Association of Independent Schools). Boston: Houghton Mifflin.

Richman, L. (1994, August). The new worker elite. *Fortune*, pp. 56-66.

Rothstein, R. (1997). *Where the money goes.* Washington, DC: Economic Policy Institute.

Roy, R. (1992, June 7). One science myth down, many to go. *Centre Daily Times* (State College, PA), p. A-5.

Samuelson, R. (1991, June 24). The school reform fraud. *Newsweek*, p. 44.

Samuelson, R. (1992, August 31). The value of college. *Newsweek*, p. 75.

Schmidt, P. (1999, July 2). A state transforms colleges with performance funding. *Chronicle of Higher Education*, pp. A26-27.

School-to-Work Opportunity Act. (1994). 103 Cong. Public Law: 103-238.

Sedlak, L. (1986). *Selling students short.* New York: Teachers College Press.

Shell Poll. (1999). Peter Hart Associates. *Teens talk about their school experience.* www.countonshell.com/ Shell.html

Shelly, K. (1992, July). The future of jobs for college graduates. *(U.S. Department of Labor) Monthly Labor Review,* pp. 13-19.

Silvestri, G. (1997, November). Occupational employment projections. *(U.S. Department of Labor) Monthly Labor Review.*

Stern, M. (1992, June 29). Employer survey. *Adult and Continuing Education Today, 22,* 25.

Sternberg, L., & Tuchscherer, J. (1992, May). Women in non-traditional careers: Setting them up to succeed. *Vocational Education Journal,* pp. 33-35.

Taylor, F. (1911). *The principles of scientific managemt.* New York: Harper & Row.

Terrell, K. (1992). Female-male earnings differentials and occupational structure. *International Labor Organization, 131*(4-5), 387-405.

Thurow, L. (1992). *Head to head: The coming economic battle among Japan, Europe and America.* New York: William Morrow.

Thurow, L. (1996). *The future of capitalism.* New York: William Morrow.

U.S. Department of Commerce. (1998, January). *Current Population Survey,* pp. 42-43.

U.S. Department of Education. (1994). *National assessment of vocational education: Interim report.* Washington, DC: Author

U.S. Department of Labor Secretary's Commission on Achieving Necessary Skills. (1991). *What work requires of schools: A SCANS report for America 2000.* Washington, DC: Author.

Walsch, M. (1994, October 12). School experts found out of sync with public. *Education Week,* p. 6.

Index

Ability, academic, 18-19, 64, 66-67
Academic middle. *See* Average
    students
Academic standards, 33, 59-61, 85
Academies, career, 122
Achievement and involvement,
    relationship between, 57-58
ACT scores, 50, 83
Admission preference, 142
Admission standards, 33, 134
Adolescent behavior, influence on,
    20-25
Adolescent career immaturity, 4,
    115-119, 180
Adrift generation, 4
Advanced placement (AP) courses,
    49, 61, 135, 138
Advanced standing, 142
Advisement, individual, 128-129
Advocacy groups, 80-82
African Americans, 37, 39
Agriculture, vocational, 48, 150
American Council on Education, 65
American Freshman Survey, 5
    (table)
American School Counselor
    Association, 120
Applied learning strategies, 164

Apprenticeships, 76, 103, 107, 135,
    146-147
Architectural engineering, 141, 151
Articulation agreement, 141
Assessment techniques, 141, 167
Assistance, individual, 128-129
Associate degrees. *See* 2-year
    programs
Automated manufacturing, 93
Average students. *See also*
    Taylorism
    academic credentials of, 54-55,
    175
    academic deficiency of, 47, 52-54,
    64
    alternatives for, 3-4, 12, 86, 107,
    176-177
    college prep program and, 49-52
    excellence for, 172-174
    high school experience of, 56-61
    high school politics and, 80-82
    limited expectations of, 59-61
    strategies for motivating, 168-
    171
    treatment of, 58-59, 153-158

Block scheduling, 167-168

Blue-collar jobs, 29-30
Budgets, school, 82
Building trades, 48, 105
Business education, 48, 150, 151

Career academies, 122
Career and technical education,
    new role of, 147, 149-152
Career choices, 112-113
Career development theories, 115-
    119. *See also* Career guidance
    program
Career guidance program:
    efforts of, 121-123, 148-149
    4-step program, parental, 124-
    129
    goals of, 113-115, 179-180
    ICP development, 119-121, 137
    individual development, 115-119
    message of, 129-131
    need for better, 111-112
    parental feedback, 123-124
Career immaturity, 4, 115-119, 180
Career information, 122-123
Career interests, verification of,
    137, 138, 179
Career planning. *See* Career
    guidance program
Career uncertainty, 58
Case study, 15-16
Clark, Burton, 31, 67
Class identification, and education,
    28-30
Clinton administration, 86
Cognitive dissonance theory, 116
College choice model, 18-19
College-level academics,
    assessment of, 49-52, 53-54
College-level jobs, scarcity of, 27,
    175-176
College mania, 7, 15-16
College prep program:
    career and technical education,
    149-152
    commitment of, 148-149

course-taking patterns, 56-61
current status of, 134-135
effectiveness of, 48-55, 64
redesign of, 135-140, 180-182
school-to-career emphasis, 143-
    148
tech prep emphasis, 140-143
Commitment, 112
Community college, 55
Competency file, 120
Computer science occupations, 14,
    40-41
Computer skills, 166-167
Construction occupations, 40, 102
Contextual learning strategies, 164
Cooperative education program,
    145
Cooperative learning, 60, 167
Core academics, 137, 143-144
Cost of education, 7-10, 99, 108-109,
    176
Counselors. *See* guidance
    counselors
Course selection options, 134, 137,
    143, 151
Craft occupations, 39, 96, 106, 177
Credentials, academic, 54-55, 61-62,
    175. *See also* Preparation,
    academic
Critical thinking skills, 137
Cultural values:
    class identification and, 28-30
    equality of opportunity, 30-32
Curriculum, academic. *See also*
    College prep program
    involvement in, 57-58
    redesign of, 133-134, 135-149,
    181-182

Dead-end jobs, 75-77
Decision making process,
    adolescents, 115-119
Degrees, future academic, 27-28
Disadvantaged youth, limited
    options for, 37-40

Discriminatory practices, 153-157, 159-160, 183. *See also* Taylorism
Downsizing, 27, 123
Drafting occupations, 40, 151
Dropouts, college, 38-39, 67-70, 175

Earnings outlook:
   for high skill/wage occupations, 30, 97, 103-106, 177
   for women, 40-42
Economic uncertainty:
   diminishing opportunities, 25-26
   labor market outlook, 27-28, 70-71
   misconceptions, 26, 94-99, 174-175
Education and status, relationship between, 28-30
Educators, school:
   high school politics and, 82-83
   limited expectations of, 156-157, 169-170
   pressure on youth, 22, 23, 183-184
Eighth-grade parents, meeting of, 125-127
Elected officials, role of, 86-87
Electrical engineering, 42
Employment outlook. *See* labor market outlook
Engineering occupations, 14, 40, 80, 106, 151, 177
English courses, 134, 137, 165
Enrollment, statistics on, 4-5, 14, 32, 33, 47
Enrollment management, 33
Equal opportunity, ideology of, 30-32
Equal status, 153-154. *See also* Taylorism
Equity audit, 159
Ethnographic case study, 81-82
External motivation, 169-170
External observers, 117
Externships, 138

Fallback skills, 150
Federal grants, 9
Financial aid, 9, 32, 34, 86
Financial planners, 88
Follow-Up Study, Class of 1998, 52-54, 56, 57, 59, 66, 147, 150
   1st-year experiences, 52-54
Foreign language courses, 134
4-year degree programs. *See also* Higher education; university graduates
   academic qualifications for, 38-39, 50-52
   analysis of, 4-7
   considerations for, 108-109
   enrollment projections, 63
   enthusiasm for, 7
Freshman, college:
   grade point averages of, 84
   remedial courses and, 64-67
   success rate of, 69, 112, 175
   survey of, 4-7
Freshman year, academic focus of, 137. *See also* Career guidance program
Funding, 9-10, 86-87
Future labor market:
   economic security and, 27-28, 70-71
   for college graduates, 71-75, 95-96
   for high skill/high wage occupations, 103-106
   for women, 40-42
   misconceptions about, 26, 94-99, 174-175

Gender barriers, 41
Gender wage gap, 40-42
General education students, 48
Gifted students, 60
Go-to-college message:
   class identification and, 29-30
   ideology of, 17-19

pressure from high schools, 22-24, 183
pressure from parents, 20-22
pressure from peers, 24-25
Gold-collar workers, 95, 96
Government aid. *See* student financial aid
Grade inflation, 84
Grade point averages, 48, 53, 84
Graduates, high school. *See also* Average students
academic credentials of, 54-55, 175
academic deficiency of, 47-52, 64
career goals of, 4-7, 17-18, 49, 79
follow-up survey of, 52-54, 57, 59, 66, 147, 150
postsecondary experiences of, 75-77
pressures on, 20-25
Graduation policies, 166
Graduation rates, 3, 9, 17, 67-70, 79
Gross domestic product, 13
Grouping system, 60, 160
Guidance counselors. *See also* Career guidance program
attitudes of, 83-84, 121, 148
high school politics and, 82-83
pressure on youth, 23

Health occupations, 107, 140, 151, 177
High-jump culture, 10-12
High schools. *See also* Career guidance program; college prep program
course selection options, 134, 137, 143, 151
discriminatory policies of, 153-156, 159-160, 183
graduation rates, 3, 9, 17
politics of, 80-82
pressure on youth, 22-24
public demands of, 84-85

social framework of, 58-59
Taylorist influences on, 156-158, 182-183
High skill/high wage occupations:
competition for, 98-99
demand for women in, 40-42
labor market outlook for, 103-106
prerequisite skills for, 39-40, 100-103, 177
rationale, 93-94, 99-100, 107, 177
Higher education:
enrollment statistics, 4-5, 14, 32, 33, 47
female enrollment in, 40
opportunity and, 30-32
remedial courses in, 65-67, 165-166, 175
revenues for, 87-88
rising costs of, 7-10, 99, 108-109, 176
state support for, 86
Hispanics, 37, 39
Home economics, 152
Homework, 60
Honors courses, 49, 60-61, 135, 138
Hossler and Stage model, 18
Household incomes, 38

Immaturity, adolescent, 4, 115-119, 180
Impoverished youth, limited options for, 37-40
Indecision, 116
Individual career plan (ICP), 119-121, 137
Individual development, decision making and, 115-119
Industrial education, 150
Inflation rate, 13
Information, career, 122-123
Information technology, 93, 104
Instructional practices, modification of, 162-168, 182

Intensive master scheduling, 167-168
Internships, 119, 138
Ivy League colleges, 80

Job openings, projected, 72 (table)
Job placement services:
  commitment of, 148-149
  school-to-career emphasis, 143-148
  tech prep emphasis, 140-143
  transitional emphasis, 138-140, 149-152, 181
Job-readiness skills, 144
Job shadowing, 119, 138, 144
Junior year. *See also* Career guidance program
  academic focus of, 140-141, 143, 144
  career development during, 119, 179

Keyboarding skills, 166
Knowledge workers, 95

Labor market myths, 26, 94-99
Labor market outlook:
  economic security and, 27-28, 70-71
  for college graduates, 27-28, 71-75, 95-96
  for high skill/high wage occupations, 103-106
  for women, 40-42
  misconceptions, 26, 94-99, 174-175
Labor shortages, development of, 13-14
Land-grant universities, 80
Learning styles, instructional practices and, 163-164
Legislation, 86

Loan interests, 86
Lobbyists, 80-82
Low-income youth, limited options for, 37-40

Majors, career, 40, 121-122
Managerial occupations, 40, 74, 105, 106, 177
Manufacturing occupations, 40, 102
Math courses, 56, 134, 137, 143, 165-166
Maturity, career, 115, 121-123
Media pressure, 24-25, 30
Medical technology, 93
Merit, 156-157
Military, 47
Minimum-wage jobs, 150
Money lenders, 88
Motivating students, strategies for, 142-143, 147-148, 168-171, 182

National Assessment of Education Progress (NAEP), 49-50
National Center for Educational Statistics (NCES) study, 5, 21, 50, 65, 174
Need-based financial aid, 34
Nonprofessional work, prejudice against, 29-30

Objective data, 126
Occupational fields. *See also* High skill/high wage occupations
  related to status, 29-30
  sex segregation among, 40-42
  supply and demand for, 71-75, 97-98
  underrepresentation among, 39-40
On-the-job training, 76, 103, 107, 145
One way to win paradigm, 4-7, 174-176

1-year certificate programs, 93
Open admissions, 19, 32-33, 87-88
Orientation meetings, 125

Parental involvement program, 125-131, 178
Parents:
    concerns of, 27-28, 139-140, 174
    considerations for, 108-109
    feedback for, 123-124
    pressure on youth, 20-22, 117
    strategies for involving, 124-131, 178
Part-time employment, 119, 138, 145
Part-time students, 143, 145-146, 147
Pathways, career, 121-123
Peer learning, 167
Peer pressure, 24-25, 117
Performance funding, 10
Performance pressure, 157
Performance skill assessment, 141
Performance standards, 59-61, 85
Personal file, 120
Personal Planning Portfolio, 120
PhD graduates, 14
Phases of youth, 115 (table)
Plan of action, 119-121
Politicians, 24, 86-87
Politics, high school:
    average students and, 80-82
    grade point averages and, 84
    guidance counselors and, 82-84
    public demand and, 84-85
    school educators and, 82-83
Portfolios, 120, 141, 167
Positive uncertainty, 117
Post-high school experiences, 52-54
Postsecondary education. *See also* School-to-career emphasis
    objective of, 107
    success of, 112-113
Poverty cycle, breaking the, 37-38

Poverty rate, 37
Pre-entrance testing, 67
Prebaccalureate emphasis, 140-143
Precision metal occupations, 39, 96, 106, 177
Preferred admissions, 142
Preparation, academic
    analysis of, 47, 52-55, 61-62
    college prep curriculum and, 48-49
    levels of proficiency, 49-52
    patterns, 56-61
Principals, high school politics and, 82-83
Private universities, financial costs of, 8-10. *See also* Higher education
Pro-Tech Program, 146
Problem solving skills, 137
Professional occupations
    class identification and, 29-30
    gender barriers in, 41
    labor market outlook for, 105, 106, 177
    supply and demand in, 70-71, 73-74
Proficiency levels, 49-52
Public demands, 84-85
Public universities, financial costs of, 8-10. *See also* Higher education

Rank-ordering, 50, 160-161
Reading skills, 49-50, 165
Recognition, 170-171
Recruiters, college, 31, 176
Reich, Robert, 123
Remedial courses:
    college dropouts and, 67-70
    effectiveness of, 38-39, 64, 65-67, 165-166, 175
Resources, educational, 184
Restructuring, economic, 25-26
Reverse transfer, 93

SAT scores, 50, 53, 54, 84

Scheduling, block, 167-168

Scholastic Aptitude Test (SAT)
scores, 50, 53, 54, 84

School administrators, high school
politics and, 82-83

School-to-career emphasis, 143-148,
181

School to Work Opportunity Act
(SWOA), 149-150

Science courses, 56, 134, 137, 143,
165

Scientific management, 156

Segregation of students, 159-160,
161-162

Self-concepts, academic, 116, 158,
170-171

Semiprofessional occupations, class
identification and, 29-30

Semiskilled occupations, class
identification and, 29-30

Senior year. *See also* Career
guidance program
academic focus of, 140-141, 143,
144, 165-166
career development during, 119,
179

Sex segregation, 40-42

Single-semester courses, 151

Skill shortages, costs of, 12-15

Skilled occupations. *See also* High
skill/high wage occupations
class identification and, 29-30
importance of, 107

Skills and wages, relationship
between, 94, 99-100. *See also*
High skill/high wage
occupations

Skills gap, 13-15

Social class and education,
relationship between, 28-30

Social expectations, 117

Sophomore year. *See also* Career
guidance program
academic focus of, 137

career development during, 179

Special needs students, advocates
for, 80-82

Specialized repair occupations, 39,
96, 106, 177

Standards, 33, 59-61, 85, 134

State funding, 9-10, 86-87

Status:
occupational fields related to, 29-
30
relationship of wealth and, 10-12
social class and, 28-30

Stereotypes, 29-30

Student financial aid, 9, 32, 34, 86

Student loan debts, 9, 69, 86, 176

Taylor, Frederick, 156

Taylorism:
defining, 155-156
influence on high schools, 59,
156-157
rationale of, 23, 157-158
strategies for ending, 159-162,
182-183

Teachers:
high school politics and, 82-83
limited expectations of, 156-157,
169-170
pressure on youth, 23, 183-184

Teaching occupations, 30

Team culture, 162

Tech prep program, 140-143, 181

Technical education. *See* Career and
technical education

Technical occupations
educational requirements for, 95-
96
labor market outlook for, 40, 104,
177
shortage of, 12-15, 80

Technical support workers, 39, 41,
106

Technology certificates, 28

Technology education. *See*
    Vocational education
Tentative career goals, 118-119, 138,
    179
Transcripts, high school, 48
Transitional academic program, 143
Transitional placement options:
    baccalaureate, 138
    honors emphasis, 135, 138
    school-to-career emphasis, 143-
        148
    tech prep emphasis, 140-143
Tuition costs, 7-10, 99, 108-109, 176
Tuition reimbursement, 148
2-plus-2 concept, 140
2-year degree programs:
    success rate of, 67-69
2-year programs:
    preparation for transfers, 47, 93
    success rate of, 67-69
2-year technical degrees. *See also*
    Tech prep program
    considerations for, 99-100, 109
    female enrollment, 41, 42
    high skill/high wage
        occupations and, 100-103, 107
    labor market outlook for, 103-106

Uncertainty, career, 58

Underemployment. *See* Labor
    market outlook
University graduates:
    above-average earnings of, 96-97
    demand for, 70-71, 97-98, 177
    labor market outlook for, 27-28,
        71-75, 95-96
    oversupply of, 98-99
Unskilled labor, class identification
    and, 29-30

Vocational education:
    enrollment in, 48, 75-77
    mission of, 103, 147, 149-152
Volunteer work, 119, 138

Wages. *See* Earnings outlook
Wealth, distribution of, 10-12
Weighted grading systems, 23, 160
White-collar jobs, class
    identification and, 29-30
Women:
    gender wage gap and, 40-42
    labor market outlook for, 74, 106-
        107
    limited options for, 39
Word-processing skills, 166
Work-based learning, 103, 144-146

CORWIN
PRESS

The Corwin Press logo—a raven striding across an open book—represents the happy union of courage and learning. We are a professional-level publisher of books and journals for K-12 educators, and we are committed to creating and providing resources that embody these qualities. Corwin's motto is "Success for All Learners."